A Celebration of Birds

The Life and Art of
LOUIS AGASSIZ FUERTES

The Book of
Louis Agassiz Fuertes

Red-breasted Merganser, *Mergus serrator*, Watercolor study, 11″ × 8½″, 1923

A Celebration of Birds

The Life and Art of
LOUIS AGASSIZ FUERTES

by Robert McCracken Peck

Introduction by Roger Tory Peterson

Published for The Academy of Natural Sciences of Philadelphia

Walker and Company ☀ New York

White-breasted Nuthatch
Sitta carolinensis
Pencil sketch
5¾″ × 8¾″

First published in the United States of America
in 1982 by the Walker Publishing Company, Inc.

Published simultaneously in Canada by
John Wiley & Sons Canada, Limited, Rexdale, Ontario.

ISBN: 0-8027-0716-5
          0-8027-0718-1 Leatherbound edition

Designed by Sheila Lynch

Library of Congress Cataloging in Publication Data

Peck, Robert McCracken, 1952–
    A celebration of birds.

    Bibliography: p.
    Includes index.
    1. Fuertes, Louis Agassiz, 1874–1927. 2. Ornithol-
ogists—United States—Biography.   3. Animal painters—
United States—Biography.   I. Academy of Natural Sci-
ences of Philadelphia.   II. Title.
QL31.F83P43   598.092′4 [B]   82-6785
ISBN 0-8027-0716-5   AACR2
          0-8027-0718-1 Leatherbound edition

Printed in Hong Kong by South China Printing Company.

10 9′8 7 6 5 4 3 2

Acknowledgements

During the research, writing, and final preparation of this book, I have received invaluable assistance, encouragement, and support from many people. I owe a special debt of thanks to my friends and colleagues at The Academy of Natural Sciences. I am especially indebted to Thomas Peter Bennett, president of the Academy, who generously provided time for me to work on this project; to Carol Spawn, manuscripts librarian, who has so competently curated the Fuertes paintings in the Academy's collection; and to Frank Gill, curator of ornithology, who patiently reviewed my bird identifications. Others at the Academy who have provided assistance are: Rob Cardillo, Andy Mack, Tracy Pederson, and Alec Forbes-Watson.

Mary Fuertes Boynton has been an invaluable source of information, inspiration, and encouragement throughout the research and writing of this book. Without her assistance, *A Celebration of Birds* could never have been written. I wish also to thank George Miksch Sutton for his help in reviewing the manuscript, and Robert Osterman for his valuable advice and editorial guidance during its final stages of preparation.

At Cornell University, where I did much of my original research, I received outstanding cooperation from everyone with whom I worked. Special thanks go to David Corson, Tom Hickerson, and Marcia Hopson at Olin Library; Wendy Owens at the Herbert Johnson Museum of Fine Art; and Linda Hooper and Charles Walcott at the Laboratory of Ornithology.

Other institutions with major Fuertes collections have also been extremely generous in their support of this project. I would especially like to acknowledge the assistance of Mary LeCroy of the American Museum of Natural History, W. Peyton Fawcett and Ben Williams of the Field Museum of Natural History, Jan Christman of the New York State Museum, Tony Newman and Marty Hill of the National Audubon Society, and Barbara Shattuck of the National Geographic Society. For sharing her own research on Abbott Thayer and Louis Agassiz Fuertes, I would also like to thank Martina Norelli of the National Museum of American Art.

Since the accurate reproduction of Fuertes' art is such an important part of this project, we are fortunate in having had the services of so many fine photographers. In addition to the staff photographers from the institutions providing illustrations for this book, I wish to acknowledge the work of Jon Crispin, who photographed all of the Fuertes paintings from Cornell University; George Eisenman, who photographed The Academy of Natural Sciences' Fuertes Collection; E. Irving Blomstrann, who photographed the two paintings from Charles Ferguson's collection; and Vincent Miraglia, who photographed the *Peregrine Falcon* in the collection of Mr. and Mrs. Scott Brooks.

The exhibition of Fuertes originals that *A Celebration of Birds* was written to accompany has been generously supported by grants from the Atlantic Richfield Foundation, the Insurance Company of North America, and the National Endowment for the Arts. The traveling arrangements for the exhibition have been made by

Marty Cappelletti of the Smithsonian Institution Traveling Exhibition Service (SITES).

I wish to thank Samuel S. Walker, Jr., and Richard K. Winslow for their enthusiastic support of this book and valuable guidance throughout its creation. Their sensitivity to the subject and general concern for quality in publishing has been gratifying indeed.

I am indebted to Sandra Smith for her careful typing of my manuscript and to all who helped to proof it during its various stages of revision.

Finally, I wish to thank E. Perot Walker for first introducing me to the art of Louis Agassiz Fuertes; my family for encouraging my interest in natural history and art; and my friends for their encouragement and support during the writing of this book.

Any errors of fact that may have slipped into the final text are the sole responsibility of the author.

Red-headed Woodpecker
Melanerpes erythrocephalus
Watercolor
10¾″ × 14″

Contents

Foreword by Thomas Peter Bennett   ix
Introduction by Roger Tory Peterson   xi

Part I   THE MAN   1
              A Quick Rise   6
              Life in the Field   11
              Home and Studio   16
              A Full-time Career   20

Part II   THE ARTIST   27
              Elliott Coues: Early Recognition   27
              Abbott Thayer: Polishing the Diamond   37
              A Painter of Life   45
              The Fuertes Style   52
              A New Departure   70
              The Later Years   90
              The Fuertes Influence   94

Part III   THE NATURALIST   99
              Alaska 1899   99
              Texas 1901   108
              Bahamas 1902   116
              Yucatan, Mexico 1910   123
              Colombia 1911   128
              Colombia 1913   135
              Abyssinia 1926–1927   139

Appendix   Chronology   162
              Major Collections   165
              List of Illustrations   169
              Notes   171
              Selected Bibliography   174
              Index   176

Harlequin Quail, *Cyrtonyx montezumae*, Watercolor, 11″ × 8½″

Foreword

Louis Agassiz Fuertes has been celebrated as one of America's greatest ornithological artists from the time his paintings were first published in 1897. While Fuertes was still a student at Cornell University, the distinguished ornithologist, Elliott Coues, observed:

> There is now no one who can draw and paint birds as well as Mr. Fuertes, and I do not forget Audubon himself when I add that America has not before produced an ornithological artist of equal possibilities.

Coues was projecting a career for Fuertes that was just beginning. Forty-five years later, Roger Tory Peterson reflected on Fuertes and his accomplishments in *Audubon Magazine* and again compared Fuertes and Audubon:

> The name of Audubon will always live in the minds of the American public. The name has become a myth, and deservedly so. Next to him, Fuertes' name will be remembered longest. To the strictly ornithological clan, [Fuertes] stands without peer, placed way ahead of Audubon. To one who knows birds, there is far more latent life in a Fuertes bird, composed and at rest, than there is in an Audubon bird wildly animated. The lay artist, unschooled in a field knowledge of birds, will insist he sees more life in an Audubon bird, but this is because Audubon strongly reflected Audubon in everything he did, whereas Fuertes reflected more the character of the bird, less of himself.

During his thirty-year career, Fuertes produced thousands of paintings and drawings for books, magazines, and private sale. Surprisingly, however, some of his best works have been unavailable to the public until now, and no integrated study of his art and its strong scientific grounding has appeared.

In 1978, The Academy of Natural Sciences of Philadelphia received more than 200 drawings and water colors by Louis Agassiz Fuertes as a long-term renewable loan from the United States Fish and Wildlife Service. Many of these works, which are remarkable for their beauty, had remained in storage almost since they were executed by Fuertes to illustrate reports by the United States Biological Survey and the Department of Agriculture. The Academy's collections include major archival and library resources in natural history art which are held in public trust, used by scholars, and exhibited to the public. The Fuertes materials, therefore, significantly strengthened the Academy's twentieth-century holdings. As well, they provided the impetus for *A Celebration of Birds,* a major exhibition of Fuertes' work which opened at the Academy in the autumn of 1982.

Under the direction of Robert McCracken Peck, a large-scale retrospective exhibition was produced. The exhibition places these new acquisitions in the context of Fuertes' artistic career, bringing together representative, and often heretofore unexhibited, works from other major Fuertes collections across the country. Peck, an art historian and naturalist, undertook the meticulous and exhaustive research required to locate and identify the most important of Fuertes' works, and to interpret these examples from both artistic and scientific perspectives. This book and the exhibition of the same title which it accompanies are the fruits of his recent labor.

A Celebration of Birds, both as an exhibition and a book, presents Fuertes as artist, explorer, and naturalist. It chronicles his development and maturation as an artist and illustrates his highly admired painting technique. Representative field studies, preliminary drawings, and final works, which had been previously dispersed, have been reunited here for the first time. These works, accompanied by the artist's field notes, letters, and journal entries, provide new insights into Fuertes' career and into the process of artistic creation itself.

Mr. Peck has been able to include heretofore unpublished works of art, documentary photographs, and letters and journal materials through the generosity of Fuertes' daughter, Mary Fuertes Boynton; the American Museum of Natural History in New York; the Field Museum of Natural History in Chicago; the Laboratory of Ornithology, the Olin Library, and the Herbert F. Johnson Museum of Art at Cornell; the New York State Museum in Albany; the National Geographic Society; the National Audubon Society, and other public and private collectors. Coupling these important new source materials with a careful selection from primary and secondary materials available at The Academy of Natural Sciences, Mr. Peck has produced what is certainly to date the most comprehensive look at Louis Agassiz Fuertes and his art.

A Celebration of Birds: The Life and Art of Louis Agassiz Fuertes will be welcomed by long-time Fuertes admirers for the fresh new insights and the comprehensive assessment it provides about this extraordinary artist-naturalist, whose works have dominated the field of natural history art for more than eighty years. Readers unfamiliar with Fuertes will be delighted by the new dimensions this book reveals about the individual and his work, and the interrelationship of art and science that Fuertes' paintings exemplify.

Thomas Peter Bennett
President
The Academy of Natural Sciences
of Philadelphia

Introduction

When I was in the seventh grade, well over sixty years ago, our teacher, Miss Hornbeck, gave each of us a small watercolor box and a color plate of a bird to copy. My choice was a blue jay from the Fuertes portfolio of *The Birds of New York State*. Eleven seems to be the magic age when so many future ornithologists become imprinted and, in my case, that blue jay did it. I was pleased with my rendering, but when it was displayed with the others on the blackboard, it was credited to Edith, who sat across the aisle. Miss Hornbeck, discovering my distress, soon put things right.

Like so many young birders of my generation, I tended to see birds as Fuertes painted them; they seemed so much more alive than those of any other bird illustrator. It was largely because of the Fuertes portraits that birds became the focus of my life—an obsession from which I have never freed myself.

In 1925, several months after my graduation from Jamestown High School, I boarded the train for New York City to attend my first meeting of the American Ornithologists' Union, which was to be held at the American Museum of Natural History. To a seventeen-year-old from a small town who had never before met any of the high ornithological "brass," the climax came when I was introduced to Louis Agassiz Fuertes.

Hanging in the bird art exhibit on the second floor of the museum were two of my own watercolors, a ruby-throated hummingbird and a kingbird. I do not remember what the master said about them, but later, to illustrate a point, he led me over to a small watercolor of a golden eagle by Archibald Thorburn, the British painter. The highlights bathing the dark back of the eagle, he explained, were actually as light in value as the shadows might be on the white breast of a gull.

As we went from painting to painting, we chatted with other well-known wildlife artists of the day: Francis Lee Jaques, who had recently been hired to paint dioramas for the museum; Charles Livingston Bull, a popular magazine illustrator; and Courtenay Brandreth, one of Fuertes' disciples. Standing before a dramatic canvas of a harpy eagle by Charles Knight, Fuertes commented that it was a pity that his friend Knight, primarily a mammal painter, painted so few birds; he did them so well. Then, stepping up to a painting of his own, a large oil of a great horned owl in a trap on the leafy forest floor, he said: "This is the way I really like to paint. . . . I'm going to do more of this from now on." This owl was not his usual brand of portraiture, but more "painterly" in execution.

When we left the hall and descended the stairs, he reached into his inner jacket pocket and withdrew a handful of watercolor brushes. Picking out a flat red sable about a half-inch wide, he handed it to me, saying: "Take this; you will find it good for laying in background washes." I thanked him, and before we parted he added: "And don't hesitate to send your drawings to me from time to time. Just address them to Louis Fuertes, Ithaca, New York."

Actually, I never did send any of my drawings to him for criticism; I had decided to wait until they were more worthy of his time. And so, by delaying, I forfeited a priceless opportunity, for less than two years later, in 1927, Fuertes met his tragic death.

Although his passion for drawing birds was sparked by Audubon, Fuertes took a new direction, bringing the art of bird portraiture to its highest degree of excellence. Even today, two generations later, most bird painters are still influenced directly or indirectly by Fuertes, although a few—like Arthur Singer—claim Audubon as their role model. As George Sutton, Fuertes' star protégé, pointed out, there was even a "Fuertes school of thinking," which extended down to the tyro who went out on Sunday with binoculars. He saw the bird briefly through his glasses, and his mind immediately went to a Fuertes drawing of that bird. He saw the bird as Fuertes drew it—with the "Fuertes look."

Visual memories are often more indelible than the written word and, although the author of a book may have his name on the cover, we tend to remember the work of the illustrator more vividly. We can easily conjure up the image of a bird in an Audubon print, but how many of us can recall what Audubon wrote about that same bird in his *Ornithological Biography*? Similarly, most of the color plates by Fuertes in *The Birds of New York* and *The Birds of Massachusetts* are well imprinted on our minds, but we have virtually forgotten the accompanying texts by Elon Howard Eaton and Edward Howe Forbush. Wildlife artists, like fine nature writers, have played no small part in the environmental movement, but they seldom receive the medals and awards that are given so freely to authors. It is significant that The Academy of Natural Sciences of Philadelphia, which has sponsored this book and exhibition, is the only major scientific institution to officially recognize this contribution with its presentation of the gold medal awarded annually for distinction in natural-history art.*

Hundreds of men and an increasing number of women have painted birds during the century and a half since Audubon. Jaques will be remembered until the museums that house his superb dioramas are demolished or rebuilt, but his more decorative canvases, reflecting the tastes of a generation ago, already seem somewhat dated. Wildlife painting has now come of age and is becoming accepted as a legitimate art form. New directions are being

*The Leigh Yawkey-Woodson Art Museum, in Wausau, Wisconsin, also presents an annual medal to "master" bird artists.

explored, but because tastes change, it is still too early to predict which of the contemporary bird artists will stand the test of time. Several are superb.

Of those who have gone before, we can be sure of only two who will be remembered far into the future: Audubon, who took birds out of the glass case for all time, and Fuertes, who really brought them to life. Whereas Audubon invariably reflected Audubon in his dramatic compositions, Fuertes caught more of the character of the bird itself—the "jizz," to use the British birders' term. No illustrator has done it better.

Although Fuertes' preeminent position in the history of art has long been recognized, and several important collections of his letters have been published, a comprehensive biography and a critical assessment of his work have long been needed. *A Celebration of Birds* fills both of these needs.

By assembling Fuertes' finished paintings with their preliminary sketches and field notes for the first time, Mr. Peck has revealed Fuertes' working methods and has provided valuable insights into his development as an artist. His extensive research into Fuertes' extraordinary life has produced a biography that is as interesting as it is informative.

It is particularly appropriate that Mr. Peck has prepared this book under the auspices of The Academy of Natural Sciences of Philadelphia, for the academy is an institution which has fostered the development of natural-history art since its founding in 1812.

This book, and the traveling exhibition which it accompanies, will undoubtedly reinforce Fuertes' preeminence in the field of bird illustration, and help to inspire a new generation of artists, birdwatchers, and all who appreciate the natural world.

ROGER TORY PETERSON

Waterfowl in flight
Watercolor
5½″ × 11″

African Fish Eagle, *Haliaeetus vocifer*, Watercolor study, 12½″ × 10½″, Abyssinia, 1927

Part I

The Man

At the annual meeting of the American Ornithologists' Union in November 1896, Dr. Elliott Coues, the foremost American ornithologist of the day, introduced to the scientific community a young artist of twenty-two on whom, he said, the mantle of John James Audubon had fallen.[1] At a time when Audubon was still lionized as the greatest bird artist of all time, such praise from a man like Coues was not to be taken lightly.

The AOU, then as now the most prestigious ornithological society in North America, had an elected membership comprised of the intellectual and scientific leaders of that rapidly growing profession. Any skepticism its members may have had about Coues' startling claims of the young man's talent had already been removed by a showing of his work at the previous year's annual congress. Now they were eager to meet the artist himself.

Louis Agassiz Fuertes, a modest but engaging senior from Cornell, arrived at the meeting in Cambridge knowing many of the members by reputation but few by sight. In three days he won the attention, admiration, and affection of everyone he met.

Frank Chapman—curator of birds at the American Museum of Natural History and editor of *Bird-Lore* magazine, and fast becoming one of the country's most influential ornithologists—was present at the meeting and took an instant liking to Fuertes. "It was one of the marvels of Fuertes' nature," he later wrote, "that much as he loved birds, he loved man more. No one could resist the charm of his enthusiasm, his ready wit and whole-souled genuineness, his sympathetic consideration and generosity of thought and deed. Everywhere he made new friends and everywhere he found old ones."[2]

So successful was Fuertes' first impression on the AOU that Coues wrote him a few days later to warn against letting the praise go to his head:

> I think you have every reason to be gratified by recent events, and am sure you had a good time in Cambridge and N.Y. Don't let this success turn your head, but just go ahead and work hard, remembering that this is but the beginning of your career, in which final success can only be achieved in the good old-fashioned way of hard work, and plenty of it, to the very best of your ability. I suppose no young man ever had a better opening; it remains with yourself to fill it, and prove that I have not said too much about you.[3]

1

Harlequin Duck
Histrionicus histrionicus
Watercolor study
8″ × 9½″
Alaska, 1899

Coues' warning was unnecessary, for Fuertes' modesty and commitment to hard work were as much a part of his character as his ability to paint.

Louis Agassiz Fuertes was born in Ithaca, New York, in 1874, the son of Mary Perry of Troy, New York, and Estevan Antonio Fuertes, a native of Puerto Rico and the son of the military governor of a hospital there. Trained at Rensselaer Polytechnic Institute in Troy, Estevan Fuertes was a professor of civil engineering at Cornell at the time of his son's birth. Later he would become dean of the Engineering College at the university.

Named after, but unrelated to, the great nineteenth-century naturalist Louis Agassiz, Fuertes was the youngest in a family of six. Of his three brothers and two sisters, only Kippy (Mary Katherine) shared his fascination with natural science. Louis and Kippy, the closest in age, kept a small private "zoo" in cages under the family's front porch. It featured an ever-changing

2

array of small orphaned or injured creatures caught in the neighborhood or given to them by friends.

As a teenager, Fuertes' interest in observing birds and animals expanded to painting, and what had begun as a method of study, quickly became a passion. He later recalled that it was in 1888, at age fourteen, when he made his "first essay at painting a bird from 'the flesh.'"[4] In a third-person autobiography written for *Amateur Sportsman* magazine in 1910, Fuertes described this historic painting experience:

> It was a male Red Crossbill—the first that he had ever seen, and the strange coppery brown of its plumage, its unbelievably queer bill, its sturdy little figure all claimed something that had never before been fully awakened. So, to fasten these peculiar qualities in his mind, where they could be retained, he followed the method that first suggested itself, and which he has followed ever since—he drew and painted it to the best of his power. It was a clumsy thing, crudely painted, awkwardly drawn standing on one foot on a drab branch of impossible anatomy—but—it was a beginning. And certainly it was a wise one, for it resulted in the production of a life's interest for the boy, which could not be diverted.[5]

That first crude crossbill sketch is now lost, but enough of Fuertes' early studies survive to confirm that his fascination with birds preceded his ability to draw them. Though busy with school activities and the diversions of adolescence, Fuertes spent his spare time studying birds, collecting specimens, and developing his artistic skills:

> . . . the study of birds and nature had to be carried on as opportunity came, along with regular schooling, and the only result was a large series of raw drawings of native birds—occasionally flowers, snakes, and squirrels—but (and here is the important thing) every one a study—as good as he could make it—from an actual specimen.[6]

Horned Grebe
Podiceps auritus
Pencil, ink, and watercolor
10″ × 13¾″
Painted prior to 1896

Although without formal art training at this stage of his development, he spent almost as much time in the library consulting the works of both writers and artists as in the field observing the intricacies of nature.

The great works of Alexander Wilson and John James Audubon enthralled him, the first for its detailed verbal accounts of North American bird life and the second for its spectacular hand-colored plates of the birds themselves. The four volumes of Audubon's magnificent double-elephant folio of *The Birds of America* (1827–1838) were in the Ithaca Public Library, and Wilson's earlier nine-volume *American Ornithology* (1808–1814), was at the Cornell library.

Although Fuertes noted in 1918 that he was "not specially concerned with the teething period of American ornithology,"[7] he admired passionately the work of these two pioneers and referred to them for inspiration—and information—throughout his life. In 1909 he wrote Witmer Stone of The Academy of Natural Sciences:

> I have always had a feeling of deep reverence and love for Wilson. [He] appeals to me as a deeper and more ardent, even if more restrained man than was Audubon. He couldn't draw with him, and he lacked the wonderful physical vigor, but he had, unconcealably, the deeper love and longing to express thro' a weaker medium, his passion for nature. . . . It [the first edition of *American Ornithology* in the Cornell University Library] was my first reference book, and meant everything to me when I was a green and longing kid, 25 or more years ago.[8]

Significantly, in mid-career he was still using Wilson's descriptions for the fugitive color parts of birds he had not been able to observe firsthand. In a 1918 letter, Fuertes refers fellow artist Bruce Horsfall to *American Ornithology,* noting that Wilson "is usually very accurate—rather more so, I have found, than Audubon—in describing these fugitive colors."[9]

Fuertes' awareness of Audubon's shortcomings, derived from his own close scrutiny of birds, in no way lessened his admiration for the naturalist-artist whose great book he described as "the most potent influence that was ever exerted upon my youthful longings to do justice to the singular beauty of birds."[10] And in 1915 he wrote:

> Say what you will of Audubon, he was the first and only man whose bird drawings showed the faintest hint of anatomical study, or that the fresh bird was in hand when the work was done, and [his work] is so immeasurably ahead of anything up to this time or since, until the modern idea of drawing endlessly from life began to bear fruit, that its strengths deserve all praise and honor, and its many weaknesses condonement, as they were the fruit of his training. . . .[11]

The impact of Audubon's plates, which Fuertes once described as his "daily bread"[12] during adolescence, may be seen in the meticulous style of his earliest paintings. Working from field observations and specimens he had collected, young Fuertes drew outlines of his subjects in ink, filled them in with watercolor wash, then highlighted the painted sections with additional

4

Bobolink
Dolichonyx oryzivorus
Wash
11″ × 8¼″

ink details. This tedious process created paintings closely resembling Audubon's hand-colored line engravings that Fuertes had admired in the library.

Compared to Fuertes' later works, these first paintings seem confining. Ink lines over watercolor create a dark, muddy appearance, while certain anatomical inaccuracies make even his most agile birds seem heavy. But, considering his age and the state of bird painting at the time he created these early works, they are of exceptional quality. Although Audubonesque in style and technique, each represents an original composition and incorporates as much behavioral information as the young artist was able to gather.

Fuertes' early insistence on working from real specimens led him to actively collect birds from the farms and woodlands surrounding his home in Ithaca. He was "pretty expert with a sling-shot," recalled his sister Katherine, "and long before he had learned to preserve skins, he would carry around birds he had shot until the carcasses or uncured skins had to be

5

consigned to the kitchen stove. First, he would cut off their wings and handle them with the utmost loving fingers arranging the webs of every feather in perfection."[13]

The young naturalist took both his drawing and his collecting seriously and by age fifteen had already sent a specimen to the Smithsonian. His parents were justifiably proud. "Louis was sixteen years old day before yesterday," wrote his mother to her eldest son, James, in 1890. "He is tall and well and filling out nicely. His bird drawings are truly beautiful. He shoots rare birds only. He never kills for fun. About two weeks ago he sent the Smithsonian a rare specimen (the farthest east it has ever been shot) and received a comment in reply requesting further correspondence and information. He feels quite set up about it."[14]

A QUICK RISE

Together, Ithaca and Cornell University formed a dynamic setting for natural-history study during Fuertes' formative years. As son of the dean of Engineering, Louis was exposed to—and known by—most of the university's faculty, including zoologist Burt Wilder and botanist Liberty Hyde Bailey. Bailey, along with artist-naturalist Anna Comstock, was soon to develop America's highly influential nature study movement.

Although Fuertes was not to work with Mrs. Comstock until later, both Wilder and Bailey actively encouraged his early interest in natural-history art. Wilder may have given Fuertes his first outside commission when he asked the seventeen-year-old to draw animals in the university's museum.

King Rail
Rallus elegans
Watercolor
15" × 21¾"
1901

Birdlike caricature
from Fuertes'
mineralogy
notebook,
Cornell University, 1897

Bailey's support, though less direct, was no less important. At a time when Professor Fuertes was growing concerned about his son's future, Bailey assured him that Louis' great interest in drawing was healthy and deserved encouragement.

The summer of 1892 found Fuertes in Paris with his family, his first major trip away from Ithaca. There, and in Switzerland where he attended school the following winter, Louis continued his bird studies. In Zurich, much of his time was spent in that city's natural-history museum, where a good-natured Swiss painter and exhibition preparator named Irniger welcomed the young American artist. Here, too, Fuertes expanded his knowledge of the great color-plate books of the nineteenth century. Where Audubon and Wilson had played such important roles at home, now John Gould, Joseph Wolf, and other European artists whose reputations matched that of Audubon, began to influence Fuertes' perceptions of ornithology and art.

Returning to New York in the fall of 1893, Fuertes entered Cornell as a freshman, quickly reestablishing his Ithaca friendships and expanding his social activity through fraternity life and participation in campus affairs.

The notebooks Fuertes kept throughout his college days say much about his interests and personality. The lighthearted caricatures of fellow students and professors that fill the margins of their pages reveal his quick wit and playful sense of humor, while the many pencil sketches of birds and mammals confirm his continued fascination with wildlife. Some of the drawings—a series of fish studies in his vertebrate zoology notebook, for example—were an outgrowth of course work, but most had nothing to do with the subjects at hand.

7

Osprey
Pandion haliaetus
Watercolor study
5″ × 8″
1897

Fuertes applied his highly developed powers of concentration to painting and ornithology with great success, but not to subjects that did not interest him. Louis' older brother, James, recalled that "Mathematics had such a soothing effect on him [Louis] that he would be asleep after about five minutes of concentration."[15] The disparate range of grades on Louis' college transcript confirms this selective focus. He did well in courses that applied to his outside interests, earning grades from 93 (vertebrate zoology) to 100 (drawing). In others his record was conspicuously worse, with failing marks in mathematics and philosophy.

Of the many extracurricular activities that Fuertes enjoyed during his college years, the glee club was perhaps his favorite. He had grown up with a love for music—an interest his mother, an accomplished pianist, had especially encouraged. Coincidentally, it was through the glee club that Fuertes first met Elliott Coues. Their meeting and the events that followed (detailed more fully in Part II) reinforced Fuertes' passion for painting birds and convinced him to transfer from Engineering to a program of Arts and Sciences during the fall of his junior year.

Coues' promotion of Fuertes' work with the scientific community and the latter's successful appearance at the AOU convention in 1896 resulted in a series of commissions that launched Fuertes' career as a professional painter of birds before he had even graduated from college. A series of pen-and-ink drawings for Florence A. Merriam's *A-Birding on a Bronco* (1896); four plates for *The Osprey,* a new ornithological magazine (1897); and 111 illustrations

8

for Elliott Coues' own book, *Citizen Bird* (1897), co-authored by Mabel Osgood Wright, were followed by other important commissions soon after his graduation in 1897. Among these were 18 illustrations for *Song Birds and Water Fowl* by H.E. Parkhurst (1897), a color frontispiece for *On The Birds' Highway* by R. Heber Howe, Jr. (1899), and a series of illustrations to be used in the AOU's own publication, *The Auk*.

Fuertes' success in launching a full-time career in bird painting without the security of an independent income was unprecedented in the United States. But, as almost everyone agreed, so was Louis Fuertes.[16] In 1897, Elliott Coues wrote to Fuertes' mother:

> I have had the handling of a good many boys who wanted to do this or that in science. I have uniformly told them that the first thing was to secure a means of livelihood . . . and to come to me again; in the matter of ornithology, when they had become self-supporting in some practical trade, business or other occupation. With Louis it is different. If things turn out as I expect, the thousand dollars or so he will put in his pocket for this work [*Citizen Bird*] is very little in comparison with what he will be able to earn soon. He should be independent of the world from the start; if his work goes on as it should, he could command more than a fair price for the productions of his pencil and brush.[17]

Fuertes attributed much of his early success to Coues. He had introduced Fuertes to many of the authors whose books he illustrated and was directly responsible for securing several of his most important commissions.

Fuertes acknowledged as his other great mentor Abbott Thayer (1849–1921), an American artist of the late nineteenth and early twentieth centuries well known for his idealized paintings of women and for his original theories

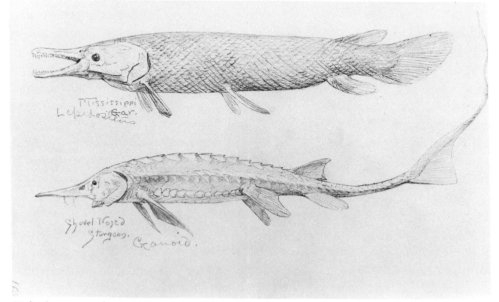

Fish drawings from Fuertes' vertebrate zoology notebook made during his junior year at Cornell University, 1895–1896.

THE AMERICAN ROBIN

" Another home bird, first cousin to the Bluebird, coming with it in the spring, and often lingering through the winter in places that the Bluebird is obliged to leave—"

" The Robin a cousin of the Bluebird !" interrupted Nat; " why, they don't look one bit alike—how can it be, Uncle Roy?"

" I expected you to ask that question," said the Doctor. " The relationship of bird fami-

AMERICAN ROBIN.

Illustration
for *Citizen Bird*
1897

on the optical properties of color and light. It was through these theories that Fuertes and Abbott Thayer first came to know each other.

As with so many of the other people who would affect Fuertes' life, Abbott Thayer met the young artist at the 1896 annual meeting of the American Ornithologists' Union. On the second afternoon of the three-day meeting, Thayer gave an open-air demonstration of his theory of the principles of protective coloration in birds. In a discussion that followed the demonstration, Fuertes suggested that brilliant male plumage of certain bird species might serve as an effective complement to the camouflaged coloration of the female by attracting predators away from the nest.

Thayer was so impressed by Fuertes' ideas that he wrote suggesting that Fuertes visit him at his home in Scarborough, New York. "What you said at the AOU in Cambridge struck me instantly as looking like new truth," he wrote. "I hope you may consent to visit me as I proposed."[18] In a hurried note a few days later, Thayer confessed that he had only just discovered that Fuertes was an artist (he had missed the display of Fuertes' work at the AOU meeting). Since his return to New York, however, he had seen reproductions of Fuertes' work in *The Osprey* and was even more eager to meet the young artist. "I can't say how peculiarly I should enjoy the company of a man doing such work as you. . . . Yours is the real thing," he wrote.[19]

Thayer was as eager to introduce Fuertes to the art world as Coues had been to expose the young artist to the scientific community, and he soon extended his invitation for a visit to an offer of free instruction during the following summer. "Somewhere in you there is a strain of very pure art and it would respond wonderfully to some pure training such as I can give you," wrote Thayer. "I want to get hold of you and swiftly develop your powers. . . . Your talent makes me itch to train it, the more because it runs to my beloved birds."[20]

10

Fuertes, still a senior at Cornell when the offer was made, may not have fully appreciated the significance of Thayer's gesture or have been aware of Thayer's stature as an artist. Although it was Fuertes' relative naiveté in academic art that attracted Thayer and gave him hope of positively influencing him, the same lack of experience made Thayer's offers of instruction less compelling than they might have been if Fuertes had been more familiar with the American art scene. Thayer addressed the issue in his letter of invitation:

> I wish you lived (more than I suppose you do) in art circles and had heard me spoken of as an authority, since my words would then have additional weight. . . .
> I trust you won't fear my influence as hostile to your individuality. I have never feared in my own case, but submitted wholly to the Ecole des Beaux Arts training, knowing that if one has the gift, it is a spring gushing out from his center, and no more to be permanently colored or muddied than a spring of water.
> I want to get you to Dublin [N.H.] and have you paint birds under my criticism as long as you can arrange to. I am asking my father to send you some clippings which he dotingly collects. I don't remember ever doing such a thing before, but I want to influence you. . . .[21]

Fuertes accepted the invitation, joining the Thayers in Dublin, New Hampshire in the summer of 1897. He quickly became a part of the artist's family. Fuertes later described this summer and subsequent visits to the Thayers' as "my happiest and most uplifting days. . . . Where would I be—and what—if I had not had them," he mused.[22]

Thayer put Fuertes through a rigorous round of academic exercises, including the tedious sketching from casts of ancient marble sculpture. "You will be amazed at the end of even a few months of pure abstract exercise of your sight power, to see how much nearer you can come to the delicate charm of a bird," he had promised Fuertes in a letter.[23]

The academic exercises interested Fuertes less than the stimulating discussions on protective coloration with Thayer. "I am merely studying, and not producing anything," wrote Fuertes to a friend during a visit with the Thayers in December 1897. "I paint every a.m., and go out into the country with Mr. Thayer and his boy every p.m."[24] The direct field observations that Thayer encouraged were to stand Fuertes in good stead in the years to come.

LIFE IN THE FIELD

Fuertes' attraction to life in the field, first evinced by his boyhood explorations of farms, woods, and deep river gorges near home, now had an important professional purpose: to observe and record the appearance, behavior, and habitats of birds. Thanks to his many contacts in the scientific community and a genial personality that made him a welcome member of any expedition, he was seldom without an invitation to travel. Beginning with a trip to Florida in 1898, he spent a part of almost every year away from home in search of birds. In thirty years, he visited five of the world's seven continents, missing only Australia and Antarctica, by the time of his death in 1927.

Fuertes relished these field experiences and the exotic places to which they took him. "You know that I was born with the itching foot," he once wrote Frank Chapman in response to an invitation to visit Colombia, "and the sight of a map—or even a time-table—is enough to stir me all up inside."[25] But while he loved the adventurous aspects of field research, he rejected "the gratuitous search for adventure" as "the bane of a working expedition."[26] As his trip journals and copious letters from the field indicate, Fuertes had no need for such search because the nature, time, and location of the expeditions he joined guaranteed adventure. His many exhilarating, and at times harrowing, experiences in the field were anything but gratuitous.

In 1899, just two years after his graduation from Cornell, Fuertes was invited to join a large, elaborate, and uncommonly luxurious scientific expedition to Alaska. It was his first major expedition and in many ways his most important.

Edward Henry Harriman, the New York financier who had recently reorganized the Union Pacific Railroad, had been advised by his physicians to take a summer cruise for pleasure, rest, and recreation. He decided to do so, not by sailing off Newport or in the Mediterranean as his doctors may have expected, but by steaming up the coast of British Columbia, down the Alaska Peninsula, and into the Bering Sea! When it became clear that the size of the boat and crew required for such a trip would greatly exceed the needs of his family, Harriman resolved to give his vacation a new purpose. In two months he changed a pleasure cruise into a scientific expedition by inviting dozens of the country's leading scientists to join him on the trip. Fuertes was included on the recommendation of C. Hart Merriam, the director of the United States Biological Survey, to whom Harriman turned for advice in assembling the expedition party. Merriam, who had first met Fuertes at the AOU congress of 1896, was the older brother of Florence Merriam whose book, *A-Birding on a Bronco*, Fuertes had illustrated three years before. Despite Fuertes' youth and relative lack of experience, Merriam was convinced that he could hold his own in such a prestigious group.

Fuertes' participation in the Harriman Alaska expedition not only exposed him to a wide range of new bird species and habitats, but also further established his place among the "movers and shakers" of the scientific and publishing world. Included among the participants in the expedition were the influential naturalist John Burroughs, the most popular natural history writer of his day; John Muir, the Sierra Club founder and America's leading conservationist; George Bird Grinnell, editor of *Forest and Stream* and one of the founders of the National Audubon Society; William H. Dall, the Alaskan explorer for whom the Dall sheep is named; Robert Ridgway, curator of birds in the National Museum and president of the AOU; Edward S. Curtis,

Semipalmated Plover
Charadrius semipalmatus
Watercolor study
8½″ × 5½″
Florida, 1898

the highly acclaimed Indian photographer; and a host of other important and influential figures. One West Coast newspaper, in heralding the arrival of the "two score eminent scientists" in Harriman's party, described the expedition as "remarkable for the number of noted men and . . . completeness of equipment."[27] Fuertes described the 126 expedition members as "a big happy family."[28]

Taking the private train provided by the Harrimans to Seattle, young Fuertes immediately established rapport with the many distinguished members of the expedition. Of the revered John Burroughs, Fuertes wrote, "He and I are like two kids in our enjoyment of the country's novelty."[29] By the end of the expedition, he would be calling Burroughs "Uncle John."

The steamship *George W. Elder,* which Harriman had requisitioned for the trip, was, in Fuertes' words, "a fine big one—250 feet long and about 40 feet wide. . . . She's fitted up in [the] finest of ways, and everybody has a stateroom to himself. Most of us young fellows are on the lower decks,

13

The S.S. *George W. Elder*, 1899

opening on the dining room. We will probably form a sort of little club to jolly the upper deckers who are either old or aristocrats or something."[30]

The expedition left Seattle on May 30, 1899 and cruised north and west, visiting Sitka, Glacier Bay, the Aleutian Islands, and Siberia. The primary geographic discoveries of the trip were a large, unknown fjord, subsequently named for Harriman, and its five live glaciers. Among the thousands of biological specimens collected on the expedition were more than 13 genera and 600 species totally new to science.[31] These consisted primarily of plants, insects, and small mammals. Although all of the western birds were new to Fuertes, they had been previously recorded by other ornithologists and could not be counted among the expedition's discoveries.

Fuertes returned from the 4,327-mile journey with over a hundred bird skins, a portfolio full of pencil sketches and watercolors, and a host of new friends, many of whom he would keep for the rest of his life. The official report of the expedition, written by John Burroughs, contained sixteen of Fuertes' bird paintings.

In contrast to the two-month Alaska trip, on which Fuertes lived in great style and comfort, the young artist's next major expedition was spartan. At the invitation of his AOU friend and fellow Alaskan traveler C. Hart Merriam, Fuertes joined Vernon Bailey, Chief Field Naturalist of the Biological Survey (now the United States Fish and Wildlife Service), and Harry C. Oberholser, assistant ornithologist for the United States Department of

14

Agriculture, on an extended field study and collecting trip in southwestern Texas in the spring and summer of 1901.

The intense heat, scarcity of food, and frequent lack of water in the remote and rugged collecting areas chosen for the expedition were all taken in stride by Fuertes, whose good humor and amiability made him an ideal traveling companion. "One morning," recalled Bailey, "Louis found one of these long-tailed whip-scorpions in his bed when he crawled out of his sleeping bag, whereupon he promptly organized the Vinegaroon Club, which no one could join who had not slept with a vinegaroon. . . . He remained the sole member." [32]

During his four months in Texas, as on his other collecting trips, Fuertes concentrated on the behavior of the birds he was planning to depict. After observing them in the field, he shot the specimens and sketched them immediately so as not to lose any of the subtle colors in their feathers or fleshy parts. He often worked long into the night, skinning and preparing birds for his fast-growing reference collection and sketching their details for his portfolio.

Fuertes' total preoccupation with his work is well demonstrated by his determined efforts to collect a zone-tailed hawk near Tornillo Creek, Texas on May 29, 1901. As Fuertes explained in a letter home, "The bird is a Texas record [i.e., a bird not previously recorded in Texas], and one of the very few U.S. records, so that when I had at last shot him, after three straight

Whip Scorpion
or Vinegarroon
Watercolor
7¾" × 10"
Texas, 1901

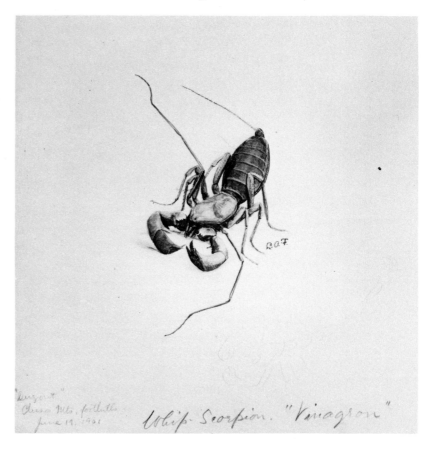

days of hunting him, it would never have done to let the splendid thing rot just because he fell over a cliff down into the canyon." The eager artist descended into the canyon and, after collecting the dead bird, tried to make his way back, but soon found himself stranded "400 feet up a 600 foot cliff," unable to go up or down. While Oberholser went off for ropes to secure his rescue, Fuertes "sat in my comfortable hole, sang to a superb echo for a while, watched lizards and ravens and got rested for an hour."[33] Undaunted by the experience, Fuertes rushed back to camp to paint the freshly collected specimen that might have cost him his life.

Despite the rather difficult working conditions, Fuertes produced some of his finest paintings during this summer in the Texas mountains. His *Black Phoebe, Vermilion Flycatchers*, and *Texas Roadrunner*, to cite only three of the dozens of paintings he made in Texas, reveal the distinctive compositional style that was already characteristic of Fuertes' work. While keeping the birds as the central point of focus and dominant feature in each painting, Fuertes skillfully arranged the background to complement his overall composition. *Black Phoebe* and *Vermilion Flycatchers* are good examples of a counterbalanced composition, where the birds and the branch form an X at the focal point of the picture. In his *Texas Roadrunner,* the horizontality of the dashing bird is reinforced by the bird's shadow and a strong horizon line, while the mountains and vegetation give a softened effect to the painting as a whole.

In each case, it is important to stress, the attitudes and positions of the birds are absolutely typical, the background terrain topographically and biologically correct. Fuertes has altered neither for artistic effect. The success of the paintings—both scientifically and artistically—lies in the artist's ability to select the most essential characteristics of the birds and their habitat and to merge them in compositions that are both accurate and visually satisfying.

While the expeditions in Alaska and Texas defined the extremes between luxury and adversity that Fuertes encountered in the field, each contained the essential elements of field research fueling his artistic creativity. These and subsequent trips, described in Part III, gave Fuertes an invaluable first-hand knowledge of birds and bird behavior, which enabled him to paint them with unprecedented veracity and life.

HOME AND STUDIO

Not all of Fuertes' travels were physically rigorous or far removed. During the summer months of his college and post-college years, Fuertes often visited a quiet summer community called Eaglesmere in northern Pennsylvania, where a large number of his childhood and college friends spent time with their families in small lakeside cottages. Fuertes enjoyed the beauty of the lake and woods, and the company of the congenial group of young people who gathered there each year. Among them was a young lady named

16

Zone-tailed Hawk
Buteo albonotatus
Wash
9″ × 6″
Texas, 1901

Margaret (Madge) Sumner from Ithaca, whose mother and stepfather, Mr. and Mrs. Dudley Finch, had rented a vacation cottage there for more than a decade.

Between scientific expeditions and periods of study with Abbott Thayer, Fuertes had been quietly courting Madge Sumner for several years, but until he had convinced himself of the economic viability of professional bird painting, he had suspended any serious thoughts of marriage. A protracted illness of his father, ending with Estevan Fuertes' death in January 1903, had further delayed any long-term personal commitments. By the summer of 1903, however, Fuertes was convinced that his future was sufficiently secure to take on family responsibilities of his own. He was equally convinced that Madge Sumner was the person with whom he wished to share the rest of his life. In August Louis proposed and Madge accepted. They announced their engagement at Eaglesmere.

After a quiet June wedding the following year, the couple sailed for Jamaica aboard a fruit company steamer on a honeymoon that tested the strength of the marriage as soon as it had begun. Never one to miss an opportunity for studying new birds, Fuertes turned the long-planned wedding trip into an ornithological expedition. Traveling by mule into the remote mountain areas of the island, Fuertes all but ignored his new wife in the excitement of finding unfamiliar species. Madge Fuertes, who did not enjoy stalking, shooting, or skinning birds, spent most of her time at a small hotel in Mandeville while her husband combed the nearby forests for birds with William Maxon, a botanist collecting plants for the Smithsonian Institution, whom Fuertes had met by chance a short time before. To his wife's dismay, when Fuertes was not in the field with Maxon, the two men were skinning, pressing, and preparing specimens in the only laboratory available to them: the newlyweds' bridal suite! It was the first and last time Madge Fuertes would accompany her husband in the field.

Despite the rocky start of their life together, Madge and Louis Fuertes enjoyed a successful, lasting marriage. They lived in half of a comfortable twin house on the corner of Thurston and Wyckoff Avenues in Ithaca just north of the Cornell campus. The three-story clapboard building had been designed and built to the couple's specifications during the fall and winter before their marriage, its construction supervised by Louis while he was still living at his family's house nearby.

For the first few years after its completion, the other half of the house was occupied by Fuertes' mother and sister, Kippy, who had helped to develop its design. When the two ladies moved to a farm in Orange County, New York, their half of the house was rented to another family.

Having had her share of life in the field during their first trip together, Madge Fuertes preferred to stay at home during her husband's subsequent trips. She understood his need to travel and never discouraged his participation in the expeditions that followed. Fuertes, a prolific and gifted letter

18

Pomarine Jaeger
Stercorarius pomarinus
Watercolor
8″ × 5″
Alaska, 1899

writer, kept her informed of his activities away from home with daily accounts of his experiences. His letters, now in the Fuertes Collection at Cornell University, are among the most evocative and compelling ever written by a field naturalist.

The Fuerteses' first child, Sumner, was born in 1905. Louis joyfully informed the Thayers of the news:

> *My dear Uncle Abbott and all My dear Thayers,* your Louis is the happiest being in this good world! Our little son came into it at a little past midnight, and my Madge is doing finely and the boy is a splendid lusty fellow, and as good and contented with his lot as if he'd picked it out for himself. . . . Kippy will tell you all about him when she comes up—in the meantime, be glad with us; for we are content beyond words.[34]

Their joy was repeated just three years later when a daughter, Mary, was born.

19

Rufous Hummingbird
Selasphorus rufus
Watercolor
5″ × 4½″
Alaska, 1899

A FULL-TIME CAREER

Fuertes' initial gamble at supporting a family on the strength of his art was now to see its greatest test. When George Sutton wrote to Fuertes in 1915, seeking advice on making a career in bird painting, he received the following reply. It summarizes the economic risks and successes Fuertes faced during the course of his career:

> . . . I realize, probably better than anyone else, because it is my *sole* profession, what its demands and emoluments are, and its risks as a livelihood. As an avocation I should put it beyond anything I know of in value: as a vocation I should certainly think long and hard, and prepare for many sacrifices in entering the lists. I have been able to command about the same annual income as I should have done as a college professor with the same grounding. I had the advantage of being early in the field, and having an excellent teacher, in Abbott Thayer, to help me to overcome my early difficulties, and an excellent executive friend in Elliott Coues, who badly needed an illustrator just as I got ripe. I have, of course, no university connection to insure me a Carnegie pension when I begin to slide down the far side. I have been lucky beyond my deserts, and I have also worked hard and long and still am. That is no hardship in a profession of such boundless opportunities for the hand and the imagination to work together. But it is not exempt from the temptation to "pot-boil," and unless you are resolved to be forever your own most relentless critic you won't be able to hold your banner high.[35]

Fortunately, Fuertes' talents proved more than adequate to provide for his family. Though their life-style was not lavish, it was certainly comfortable.

20

The Ithaca house, in which they lived until after Louis' death in 1927, was the center for family activity ten months of the year. In July and August, however, Louis, Madge, and the children would move to a quiet summer retreat called Sheldrake Point on Lake Cayuga, twenty miles north of the city.

For the first summer or two, Fuertes tried to paint at Sheldrake, but as temperatures were warm and distractions many, he decided to spend the time with his family and friends instead, relaxing and recharging his energies for the ensuing fall. During the summer of 1916, George Sutton, who eventually became Fuertes' best-known pupil and protégé, spent several weeks with the Fuertes family, watching his mentor complete work on a *National Geographic* commission for "The Larger North American Mammals." It was one of the few summers Fuertes brought his work with him to Sheldrake.

For various reasons he preferred to paint in his home studio, with easy access to the extensive collection of study skins he had gathered during many field trips in the United States and abroad.

In 1913, after a fire in his third-floor studio, Fuertes constructed a separate fireproof structure to serve as studio, workshop, and storage place for his collections. The main room of the building, with its fireplace, bookshelves, cabinets, and intriguing array of souvenirs from early expeditions, quickly became the center of his professional life. There, at a large table beside a six-by-nine-foot northern window—and surrounded by Indian blankets, mounted birds, skins, cartoons, sketches, and anthropological artifacts from around the world—he painted more bird portraits than any artist had ever

Fuertes at work on a whooping crane painting in his Ithaca studio, c. 1923.

before attempted. "When I started," he once explained, "there wasn't any field [of professional bird painting], but one developed, and now there is considerably more of a one than one man can fill."[36]

The demand for Fuertes' paintings came from most of the leading natural history writers of the period. John Burroughs, Frank Chapman, Thornton Burgess, William Beebe, Anna Comstock, and Edward Howe Forbush were among those who asked him to illustrate their books. The editors of *National Geographic, St. Nicholas, Country Gentleman, Outing,* and other widely read national magazines also commissioned illustrations. In all, during the thirty years of his professional career, Fuertes prepared illustrations for more than thirty-five books and approximately fifty educational leaflets, handbooks, and bulletins. He was a regular contributor to more than a dozen popular and scholarly journals.

Fuertes occasionally accepted advertising projects, too. The most successful, and perhaps the best known, was for the Church and Dwight Company, distributors of Arm and Hammer Baking Soda. In the 1920s, for his friend and fellow conservationist Charles T. Church, Fuertes painted some ninety bird portraits. The plan was to include a reproduction in each package of baking soda. There were three series of thirty studies each: song birds, game birds, and birds of prey. These small reproductions were collected as avidly as baseball cards—especially by children—and did much to increase public knowledge of ornithology.

Through books, magazines, and advertising promotions, Fuertes' accurate and appealing depictions of birds were given such wide distribution that, for many, his paintings became more memorable than the birds themselves. As Roger Tory Peterson observed in 1942, the average bird-watcher of the period would see a bird "as Fuertes drew it, not as it actually looked in the brief moment it perched before him."[37]

Louis Fuertes' quick rise in the field of bird painting may be attributed, in part, to his being introduced early to the proper scientific and publishing circles, but certainly the most important reason for his success was his innate artistic talent. At a very young age, Fuertes surpassed all of his contemporaries in the field. The best-known was Canadian naturalist-artist Ernest Thompson Seton. (He was actually born Ernest Seton Thompson, but for a number of family reasons reversed the order of his names several times, legally becoming Ernest Thompson Seton in 1901.) Seton, an enthusiastic outdoorsman who helped to establish the Boy Scouts of America, was a prolific writer, illustrator, and popularizer of natural history.

At the time Fuertes was just beginning his professional career in the late 1890s, Seton's paintings, stories, and reputation were everywhere. Despite an inevitable competition for artistic commissions, however, no evidence exists to suggest that Fuertes and Seton ever considered they were rivals. Perhaps to avoid such an impression, the two men went out of their way to recognize each other's talents. Seton took the first step in this regard by inviting the younger artist to join an expedition to Manitoba in the spring of

22

1901. Frank Chapman, who described Seton as the "originator" and himself the "executor" of the trip, took special pains to inform Fuertes that he, Fuertes, had been invited at Seton's request.[38] Unfortunately, Fuertes' survey work in Texas ruled out his participation in the trip.

Years later, when Fuertes was working on "The Smaller North American Mammals" for *National Geographic*, he called upon Seton's expertise to provide illustrations of animal tracks for the article. In a subsequent letter to Gilbert Grosvenor, editor of *National Geographic*, he modestly sidestepped discussion of his own drawings and praised Seton's contribution as "one of the most interesting features in the whole article."[39]

Although Seton never publicly acknowledged Fuertes' superior abilities in depicting birds, it is significant that soon after Fuertes appeared on the scene, Seton redirected his attentions, in both painting and prose, to the field of mammals (an area as yet untried by Fuertes), producing dozens of enormously popular books on the subject.

Though their personalities differed in many ways—Seton was often considered conceited, egotistical, and self-serving—their interests and careers frequently overlapped. Both were very devoted to and active in the Boy

Canada Geese in flight
Branta canadensis
Watercolor
15½" × 22"

23

Downy Woodpecker

Fuertes' bird paintings were featured on three series of small (3″ × 1¾″) collector's cards offered in boxes of baking soda during the 1920s, '30s, and '40s. Descriptions on the back of each card provided information about the birds.

Scouts. Both worked for the United States Biological Survey and for the American Museum of Natural History. Both illustrated editions of Frank Chapman's *Birds of Eastern North America* and produced illustrations for *Bird-Lore, St. Nicholas,* and *Outing* magazines (to name only a few). The most important bond between them, however, was a common insistence on basing their work on firsthand field observation.

Another Canadian artist with whom Fuertes had much in common was Allan Brooks. Fuertes first met the talented and genial Brooks in 1920, soon after Brooks had returned from the war. Having admired each other's work for years, the two men were delighted when Frank Chapman and T. Gilbert Pearson arranged to bring them together at the Cosmos Club during the AOU annual congress in Washington, D.C. "We had such a talk fest," Brooks recalled of their first meeting, "that we missed the first part of the members meeting."[40] Fuertes invited Brooks to visit him and his family in Ithaca—Brooks did, from November 24th to Christmas Day, 1920—and then joined him for a trip to Florida early in 1921. The two became fast friends and greatly enjoyed the stimulation of personal and professional discussions. In a letter to Brooks the following fall, Fuertes urged his new friend to accept any commission he might receive from Edward Howe Forbush, who was then organizing a huge publication, the *Birds of Massachusetts and Other New England States.* Fuertes had been selected as the primary artist but, happy to share the commission with Brooks, he wrote, "I wouldn't want to cooperate with Brasher or Horsfall, but would be honored and pleased to join with you on it."[41]

Unlike Brooks, Fuertes frequently had more work than he could handle. When this occurred after 1920, he tried to turn commissions in the direction of his Canadian friend. A recommendation he sent Gilbert Grosvenor in 1924 reflects the admiration he felt for Brooks and his work:

> Major Allan Brooks, of Okanagan Landing, British Columbia, is just as capable as I am—if not more so—to undertake this commission and I haven't the slightest hesitancy in suggesting that you get into touch with him, outline your general idea, and ask him to undertake it. He is a bird-painter with wide experience, a delightful interpretation and close knowledge of wild life, having lived for the past 35 years in western Canada, close to nature, and having thus attained a wholly sound and solid viewpoint, and having also painted assiduously. In England he is far better known that I am, and this is also true of the west in this country where he has a "grade A.A.A." reputation as a painter of birds. The past year he has been working in California, on the birds of that State, having finished and gone back to Okanagan just after Thanksgiving. I feel quite sure he could undertake it, having just completed a big work and

now taking a little rest. As to his output, he works quite as fast, and certainly achieves fully as good a result as I do, so I do not hesitate a moment in suggesting that you ask him to undertake it.[42]

Unfortunately, his recommendations were not always accepted, as a letter from the Forbes Lithograph Manufacturing Company of Boston reveals:

Dear Mr. Fuertes:
  Your letter of the 26th received, for which many thanks.
  We appreciate your suggestion of Mr. Brooks, and admire your testimonial of his ability, but without intending any flattery we frankly say that, to the general public, there is no one who can take the place of Fuertes. . . .[43]

The painting styles of the two men were somewhat similar when they first met, but drew closer after their period of shared experience. Fuertes became interested in Brooks' use of colored paper and opaque paint—a technique he had also admired in Archibald Thorburn's paintings. Brooks, in turn, picked up some of Fuertes' lightness and spontaneity of pose. In the several publications they jointly illustrated—most notably, John C. Phillips' *A Natural History of Ducks* (1922–1926) and Edward Howe Forbush's *Birds of Massachusetts and Other New England States* (1925–1927)—Brooks and Fuertes moved consciously closer in style, hoping to achieve uniformity for the books involved.

Despite the unparalleled success of his scientific illustrations, in the mid-1920s Fuertes began to experiment with more inventive compositions. He indicated to his friends and family that when his current commissions were completed, he intended to devote more time to painting for its own sake.

Several private works of Fuertes completed during this period, and a large number of field studies he made during an expedition to Abyssinia (now Ethiopia) sponsored by the Field Museum of Natural History and the *Chicago Daily News* in 1926–1927, give an idea of the exciting new direction his art was taking at the time of his death. A bold, loose handling of paint and a freer compositional style characterize the paintings of this period. We can only imagine what Fuertes' genius might have produced had he lived another decade.

In August 1927, shortly after his return from Abyssinia, Louis Fuertes was killed when his car was struck by a train at a grade crossing near Unadilla, New York. He and his wife were returning from a visit with the Frank Chapmans, to whom Fuertes had been showing his Abyssinian paintings. His wife was injured in the accident. The paintings, miraculously, were thrown clear of the wreck.

During a memorial service for Fuertes a few months later, Chapman stated:

If the birds of the world had met to select a human being who could best express to mankind the beauty and charm of their forms, their songs, their rhythmic flight, their manners for the heart's delight, they would unquestionably have chosen Louis Fuertes.[44]

Fuertes himself could not have asked for a finer tribute.

Eastern Kingbird

White Gyrfalcon, *Falco rusticolus*, Watercolor, 21″ × 15″

Part II

The Artist

In the long history of bird painting, the name of John James Audubon has come to symbolize the pinnacle of popular success, for his work has been more widely reproduced and is therefore better known than that of any other bird artist. Such domination of the field has established Audubon's work as the standard against which all others are judged.

Predictably, from the time of its first publication, Louis Fuertes' art has been compared to Audubon's.[1] Almost unanimously, Fuertes has been named the superior artist. Since the two men represent significantly different eras in the history of ornithological illustration, such comparisons prove little, except in the discussion of specific stylistic influences and similarities. The frequency with which comparison is made, however, is significant, for it suggests a consensus of thought on Fuertes' stature as an artist. However meaningless they may be in themselves, the favorable comparisons represent a recognition of Fuertes' own status as a standard setter.

In light of his unparalleled talent and affection for the subject, Fuertes' decision to make a profession of bird painting seems perfectly logical to us today. But at the time, it was a bold decision running counter to his parents' wishes and to all arguments of economic practicality. His family tolerated his interest in birds and bird painting as a pleasant pastime, but Fuertes' father was eager to have him take up some more gainful profession, such as architecture or engineering. With that objective, Fuertes entered Cornell as an engineering student in 1893. In the middle of his sophomore year, however, he made a drastic career choice and launched himself on a professional course without precedent. He attributed the impetus for the decision to the influence of one man.

ELLIOTT COUES: EARLY RECOGNITION

As with many momentous events, it came about almost by chance. During the planning of a concert tour in December 1894, Louis' fellow glee club member Charles Henrotin mentioned that he had an uncle living in Washington, D.C. who was "crazy about birds." Henrotin offered to introduce the two while the glee club was visiting the capital and suggested that his friend take some of his best paintings along. Fuertes would have enjoyed meeting a fellow bird enthusiast in any case, but when he learned that the uncle was Elliott Coues, America's preeminent ornithologist, he must have been overwhelmed with excitement. An associate member of the American Ornithologists' Union since the age of seventeen, Fuertes was well acquainted with the work of the Union's founder. Coues' *Key to North American Birds,* first published in 1872, had long been recognized as the most important book on American birds since Audubon's opus of forty years earlier.

No account of the meeting between the two men has survived, but subsequent letters from Coues indicate that for Fuertes, it was a triumphant success and the pivotal point in the development of his career. "Ever since that first interview with Coues," he wrote, "[I] never thought of adopting any other profession."[2] At least in part, it was thanks to Coues' early support that he would never need to.

In a letter following their first meeting, Coues requested more pictures to criticize and casually mentioned that he was sharing the young artist's work with Audubon's granddaughters. This was incentive enough for Fuertes to produce some of his finest paintings to date. Working on large sheets of heavy white bristol board, he produced a series of finely arranged compositions of two or more native birds—usually male and female of the same species—amidst branches and leaves of appropriate native vegetation. Although still emulating Audubon in style, Fuertes had abandoned the meticulous ink outlining of his earlier work. A letter to a young artist written later in Fuertes' career suggests that the reason for this change of technique may have been due to physical necessity as much as to artistic preference:

> Right at the very first I'm going to tell you to drop pen and ink as a medium, and stick to pencil and brush. The reason is this: in pen and ink your tones all have to be made by the sharp contrasts of black and white—just about the most trying test for the eyes that could be devised. I can work in color or in pencil for weeks and never notice the slightest eye-strain: one hour with pen and ink gives me a head-ache and makes me so sorry for myself that I'm no good to anybody. So I long ago threw it out, as eyes are the greatest possession as well as the greatest need of anybody who takes up any graphic art seriously. . . . Pen and ink so strains the eyes of most people that it might best be left for the few with cast-iron eyes who can do it without bad results.[3]

Two striking portraits of warblers completed in May 1895 were undoubtedly among the group of watercolors Fuertes mailed to Coues before leaving for England and Europe with the Cornell Glee Club in June. They prompted Coues to write:

Dear Mr. Fuertes:—
> The paintings are safely to hand, and much admired. Your improvement in the technique is marked, and I am more than ever hopeful that I may be able to bring you out a little later.
> Have a good time abroad, but always keep your eyes open for anything in the way of bird art and artists, and let me hear from you again.
> With regards,

Very truly your friend,
Elliott Coues[4]

Chestnut-sided Warbler
Dendroica pensylvanica
Watercolor, ink, and pencil
14½″ × 9″
1895

Chestnut-Sided Warbler.
Dendroica Pensylvanica (Linn.)
Male and Female.
May 10th 1895.

The contents of Fuertes' travel sketchbooks from his summer's trip show how closely he heeded Coues' advice. His pencil drawings of Bateleur eagles and a sleeping lioness in the London Zoo, and of a number of birds from the Hanover Zoo, reveal Fuertes' well-developed draftsmanship and ability to capture lifelike poses. His informal sketches of traveling companions suggest his versatility as an illustrator and his popularity among the members of the club.

During the fall of 1895, Fuertes continued to send paintings to Elliott Coues who, in turn, showed them to his own wide circle of friends. By

November, Coues had a large collection of paintings that, in the artist's absence, he exhibited to the members of the American Ornithologists' Union, then holding its annual congress in Washington. In a letter of November 14th, the closing day of the meeting, Coues sent Fuertes the following report:

Dear Mr. Fuertes:—

According to my promise I brought your name prominently before the American Ornithologists' Union by exhibiting about fifty of your best paintings and talking about them. You would have felt proud and pleased if you had been present to see how highly they were praised by many besides myself. I hope you are persevering under competent instruction in certain points of technique, and that in the end the result will be that I can bring out for you a very handsome volume of colored plates, and thus secure for you a permanent reputation.

Sincerely your friend,
Elliott Coues[5]

The response to Fuertes' introduction was immediate. Frank Chapman queried the young Cornell student about doing illustrations for his forthcoming *Bird-Life*. Florence Merriam wanted plates for a book on western birds, and Walter Adams Johnson sought pictures for *The Osprey*, an ornithological magazine he had recently started.

Carrying a full course load of seven classes and extracurricular commit-

Bataleur
Terathopius ecaudatus
Pencil study
London Zoo, 1895

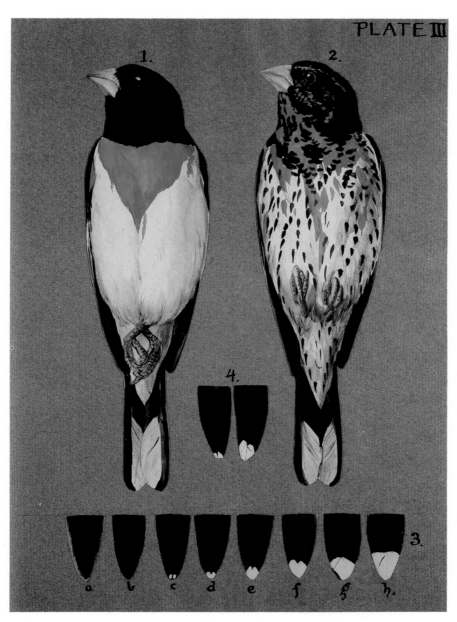

PLATE III

A page from Fuertes' senior thesis on coloration in birds depicts adult and immature male rose-breasted grosbeaks *(Pheucticus ludovicianus)* and a gradation of markings in tail feathers. The watercolor was made in 1897.

ments in the glee club and the *Cornell Widow,* a college humor magazine he had helped to found, Fuertes would have been hard-pressed to fill all three commissions during his junior year. He was probably disappointed but relieved, therefore, when Chapman redirected his commission to Ernest Thompson Seton. The other two assignments he accepted with enthusiasm. The publication of Miss Merriam's *A-Birding on a Bronco,* in the following

31

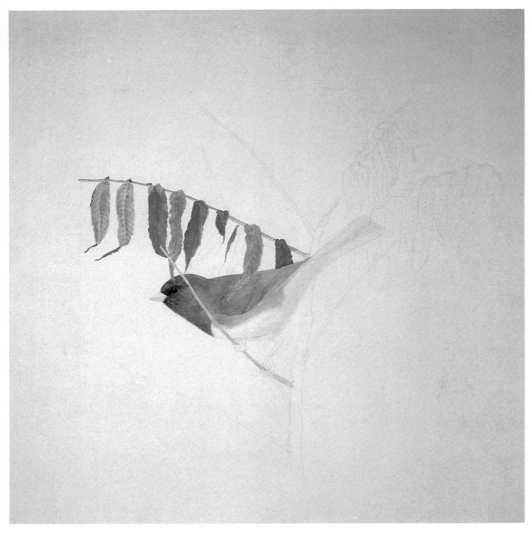

Slate-colored Junco
Junco hyemalis
Watercolor and pencil
18¼″ × 14½″

year, elicited a review in the *New York Nation* by Elliott Coues, which concluded with this assessment of Fuertes' contribution to it:

> We notice this booklet mainly to call attention to some of the pictures it contains. About a year ago we had occasion to speak of some artistic work done by Mr. Louis Agassiz Fuertes, a student at Cornell University, whose paintings of birds were much admired when exhibited before the A.O.U. at its last meeting in Washington. He is self-taught, and his technique is still crude, he needs disciplining to keep him from straining for effect; but his power is unmistakable, and we miss our guess if he does not become a great artist in birds in due course, if he perseveres. Thus far his genius overreaches his talent; but his pictures are better than Audubon's were to begin with, and we suspect that the mantle has fallen upon Mr. Fuertes. . . . Ability to draw a live bird instead of a stuffed one, from the very first, is an accomplishment rare enough to deserve more than passing comment.[6]

Coues, who had talked about publishing Fuertes' work from the time of their first meeting, provided his young friend with an important commission

32

in the fall of 1896. Coues and Mabel Osgood Wright were writing a children's book called *Citizen Bird*. Here was Coues' opportunity to further expose Fuertes' talents to the public and simultaneously enhance the appearance—and sale—of his newest book. He informed Fuertes of his plans in September:

> You will no doubt soon receive from Macmillan Company of New York a very important letter, in regard to making about one hundred drawings of birds for a work which they will publish, and of which I am one of the authors; and if you send me the letter, I shall be in position to advise you how to reply to it. The publishers' choice lay between you and an artist of recognized ability and secure reputation; and I have such confidence in you that I have secured the offer for you. If this proposed arrangement can be made, and the result prove satisfactory, you will have been fairly started on the road to fame and fortune.[7]

House Sparrow with feathers
Passer domesticus
Watercolor
14″ × 10″

Pileated Woodpecker
Dryocopus pileatus
Watercolor study
8¼″ × 6″
1898

Pileated Woodpecker

Grant = March 30-98=

During the next eight months, in addition to accomplishing his school-work and other activities, Fuertes managed to produce 111 drawings for Coues. Each had to comply with the author's exacting standards, and more than one was returned for reworking:

As I think I told you in N.Y., I will accept all the pictures you showed us, with the two exceptions of the nuthatch and the hummingbird, which I should like to have you do over again. Put the nuthatch in the most characteristic attitude, head downward on a perpendicular tree trunk, with a full rounded breast, and bill pointing horizontally out to right or left. Take the frame work away from the hummingbirds, set the ♀ better on the nest, and draw the bills thinner.

34

And in general, *keep your accessories down*. What we want is the *bird*, with least possible scenery, stage setting, framework or background of any description. You will remember that even in the cases of those very fine pictures of the summer warbler and the yellow-rump, the *foliage* about them somewhat interfered with the effect. Be always careful about this.[8]

But Coues, who took a paternal interest in Fuertes' career, always coupled his criticism with praise:

Feb. 6, 1897

Dear Mr. Fuertes:—

I have your 16 new drawings. They are beauties indeed. You seem to improve with each new effort. You are now mastering the technique, and getting such a grasp on your art that I think by the time you have done the present lot there may be no one now living, except perhaps Wolf, who will be able to draw birds as well as you do. The gem of this lot, to my eye, is the Night Hawk and moth—a bold conception, artistically executed. The Whippoorwill is very fine, and so are both the hawks.

Don't get your head turned or swelled, go steady now, patiently, laboriously, faithfully, with the most scrupulous care for precision in every minute detail—this is talent; but at the same time give your genius its own scope and free play, in conceiving attitudes, actions, and accessories; yet, keep the accessories wholly subservient to the main figure—the bird.

I heartily approve this lot, with no criticism except in one case. You must do the Turnstone over again. It is good, but not up to your present mark; for you have relapsed into your early crudeness about the belly and legs. I noticed in your early drawings of the water birds that you had not learned to handle these parts. Now you have got the Plover on its legs just right, and you must remodel the Turnstone to make it stand as the Plover does. At present the Turnstone has got its legs pulled out about an inch too far. It would pass muster with ordinary drawings, but is not up to your own mark, and you must either fit it with a new pair of legs, or draw another altogether. You see how solicitous I am that nothing whatever shall appear in these drawings to detract from your highest standard of excellence.

I return the drawings, and have written to Mr. Brett about them.

You may like to see the enclosed, which corroborates your remarkable picture of the Chimney Swift.

Very truly yours,
Elliott Coues[9]

The additional work extended Fuertes' association with the project well past the original February deadline. It affected his academic performance unfavorably as the spring of his senior year approached, and Professor Fuertes pressed Louis for better grades. Elliott Coues, however, urged him back to the drawing board. "Never mind your school work," he wrote. "What matters is what you are doing for me."[10]

Such admonitions may seem harsh and blatantly selfish in retrospect, but Coues did not see them in that light. Clearly, he considered Fuertes' genius

something, and cannot exactly sing. Johnny and Jenny make a great fuss, but they are really very fond of each other and make the very best of citizens, eating no fruits and being officers in the guilds of Ground Gleaners and Tree Trappers."

"Look!" said Dodo, "Jenny is scolding and dancing about, and Johnny is singing away again. What is the matter with them, Uncle Roy?"

"Did you never hear the 'Wrens' duet'? That is what they are singing now. Listen, and I will tell you what they say in House People's language:

Johnny (keeping time with his wings):

HOUSE WREN.

Illustration for *Citizen Bird* 1897

in painting far more important than the formality of a degree. His opinion of the relative merits of Fuertes' activities is revealed in a letter of 1897, in which he reports the public reception of his book *Citizen Bird*:

> It is well that you are an alumnus—an A.B., or B.S., or whatever it is. But that is not a circumstance to your accomplishment in Citizen Bird, through which you have made, at a single bound, a reputation that most artists struggle painfully for during many weary years of working and waiting for recognition and mere livelihood. The book was out on the 14th, and is a phenomenal success at the start, with a sale averaging 500 copies a day. We expect to do still better as trade revives in the fall. This great hit is mainly due to your pictures, which I consider the finest series of 108 bird portraits ever printed in black and white. The book sells on sight—almost everybody that sees it wants a copy, and it is sure to be immensely popular.[11]

Fuertes received the news of the book's great success in Dublin, New Hampshire, where he was spending the summer as a student-in-residence with artist Abbott Thayer and his family. Thayer's generous offer to instruct Fuertes, which evolved from discussions between the two at the preceding year's American Ornithologists' Union congress, was to have as much impact on Fuertes as his introduction to Elliott Coues. Coues could advise on the scientific aspects of Fuertes' work, but Thayer would bring to it an artist's perspective. Fuertes recognized the value of this balance and observed, quite rightly, that he "now had the help of the two most effective friends he could have found"[12] in developing his talents as a painter of birds.

ABBOTT THAYER: POLISHING THE DIAMOND

In Abbott Thayer, Louis Fuertes found a generous friend, a stimulating teacher, and a powerful and extremely complex personality. An artist renowned for his idealized depiction of women and children, Thayer was, at the same time, an exacting naturalist with an obsession for visual accuracy. Sensing a kindred spirit in Fuertes and praising his painting as "the true thing," Thayer insisted on his coming to New Hampshire. "Your talent makes me itch to train it," he wrote. "I want to get you to Dublin and have you paint birds under my criticism. . . . I am not sure that you yet know that the highest art-purity is needed in your birds. If [not] so, you will ultimately believe it. All that true training does is to purify one's powers, till they no longer refract the truth in its passage through."[13]

The warm atmosphere in the artist's home and studio, often compared to Eden and dubbed "Thayerland" by those who knew it well,[14] reflected Thayer's contagiously positive outlook on life. Yet there was a dark side to this happiness. On occasions, fits of depression marred Thayer's generally euphoric state. Although such changes of mood rarely involved Fuertes,

Fuertes with Thayer children and friends, 1902. (l to r: Gerald Thayer, Margel Gluck, LAF, Clair Gluck, Gladys Thayer)

they did eventually contribute to Thayer's rejection of Fuertes during a period of deep melancholia just before Thayer's death in 1921. Nothing could have been more painful for the younger artist, who was deeply devoted to Thayer and his family. Ironically, the breach between them revolved around the very principles that had fostered and nourished their close personal and professional ties.

Concealing coloration in birds, a subject that preoccupied Thayer for much of his life, was the topic of his address to the AOU congress of 1896, when Fuertes and he first met. Previously, Fuertes had developed a number of similar theories on his own. In his Cornell senior thesis on the coloration of birds, he combined the two parallel lines of thought, highlighting the paper with original watercolors of birds and bird plumage to strengthen his points. While the paintings probably came more easily to Fuertes than the text they were drawn to illustrate, the writing exercise was a valuable experience. It helped him to crystallize his ideas about a complex subject that would touch every aspect of his career. It also provided the best possible preparation for his summer with the Thayers.

When Fuertes first visited the Thayer household, it consisted of Mr. and

Pied-billed Grebe
Podilymbus podiceps
Pen and ink
7″ × 10″

Mrs. Thayer (soon Uncle Abbott and Aunt Emma to Fuertes); Mary (called Je-je), twenty-one; Gerald (Gra), thirteen; and Gladys (Galla), eleven. "It was an instantaneous friendship," wrote Gladys later:

> He boarded in the village and we saw him about every day. We youngsters glowed in his fun-making, as we did in his brilliant work. . . . He delighted impromptu outdoor audiences by his uncanny ability to summon long missing 'bird neighbors' which some of these folks lamented not having been around for years! We all had great wood-walks, camping, etc. . . . Of course, my dad (who worshipped his astounding power of putting the very soul into the birds or animals which he re-created with such speed) did give him regular criticisms of his work. It was usually restricted to 'values' of light and shade, my dad pointing out how the picture would be improved by 'flattening' as artists call it. We youngsters would often have to run for the salt cellar, some of whose contents Papa would thinly sprinkle over the painted bird!
>
> While applying himself to a picture-task in his room, (using sometimes a freshly-shot bird, of whatever kind, to guide him in his miraculous rendering of the bird in life, sometimes a duck or other bird bought in a New York market) no sound would be heard during the two or three morning hours while he worked. When a sudden blast of melodious whistling filled the house, we could be sure the picture was finished, and he would soon bring it down.
>
> Many were the walks, and campfires in the twilight woods, that we enjoyed with him.[15]

Fuertes spent the summer of 1897 in Dublin and the following winter in Scarborough, N.Y. (Thayer's winter residence), observing from nature and recording on paper the effects of light and color. His purpose—and Thayer's—was to improve painting skills, not to produce paintings; to conduct his studies without the pressures or psychological inhibitions associated with completing finished works. In Fuertes' letters to other aspiring artists, written years later, we can almost hear the advice Thayer must have given Fuertes in the fall of 1897:

> Work all for study, and none for either exhibition or commendation, at least for a while. As long as you fear criticism, you will hedge at making experiments and downing tradition. So don't work for anything but your own progress.[16]

> Painting is *easy* after you've learned sight, and a painter's greatness is far less dependent on his ability to handle paints and brushes than on his ability to rightly see the truth. Probably the hardest thing of all, at first, is to get rid of prejudices—or mental habits, to the effect that because a pine tree for instance, is *known* to be blue-green it always looks that way, regardless of lighting conditions. Get out of the notion that black is always black—or that any other color is always true to its name. Colors have no such loyalty, and if something you know is green *looks* violet, don't be afraid to so paint it. Be honest with yourself—go ahead—your mistakes will teach you more than your successes if you have the honesty and courage to *use* them and not discard them as failures. It is through study of mistakes that they are not repeated: success *may* be largely luck, whose elements are unrecorded and consequently not available next time you need them.[17]

39

Tree Sparrow, *Spizella arborea,* Watercolor, 15″ × 11¾″, 1898

During his open-air lecture at the AOU congress in Cambridge, Thayer dramatically demonstrated one of his principles of protective coloration in the natural world. He hung three sweet potatoes on a wire stretched horizontally a few inches from the ground. Next, he coated the potatoes with a sticky substance and sprinkled them with dust from the road over which they were displayed so that they would match the color of their surroundings. Then he painted two of the potatoes white on their undersides, working the paint gradually into the brown of the sides. Contrary to the expectations of his audience, the painted potatoes were, from a distance, quite invisible, while the third appeared in strong relief against its background, its shadow creating a darker appearance on the lower half of the sphere. This effect, in turn, made the entire potato seem much darker than it was.

Thayer conducted a similar experiment with green and white paint on potatoes over grass, to the same effect. The two demonstrations convinced viewers of the validity of Thayer's claim that terrestrial birds and mammals achieve a protective invisibility by similar countershading principles.

Fuertes' own experiments had brought him to the same conclusion, and he spent much of his life demonstrating the principle and trying to convince others that it was valid. A 1915 letter to George Sutton states his opinion on the subject and reveals, perhaps, something of his own study methods during the Thayer years:

> . . . take a bird with a white belly and study, locally, the color of its shadow on the white. Put colored things so they can reflect in this shadow, and see what a mirror of adjacent colors white becomes in shadow. Your shadows lack in both color and in depth. It would be good exercise to paint, literally, a birdskin or a dead bird, with the one aim of getting every point on it in exactly the proper relation in both color and value (value equals the relative amount of lightness and darkness, irrespective of color) to every other point. This will give your object—or bird in this case—solidity and rotundity, and is the only thing that will. . . .

To take an example, let us analyze the fall magnolia warbler picture. Your drawing is nice, the conception pretty, graceful and very characteristic. The coloring is, locally, correct. But it so happens that local color (by which I mean the exact tone and color of a given part of the bird, seen in most favorable and analytical light) only tells at its face value and color rarely. On top, where much light hits it and sprays off, it is greatly lightened and 'greyed'; underneath, where an inevitable shadow falls, it is greatly darkened, and also reflects color and life from surrounding objects. If you realize at once what it has taken students all these centuries to wake up to; namely that *all* animals that are dark on top and pale below are so for the sole purpose of overcoming or compensating this inevitable top light and bottom shadow, your main difficulty will be solved. It is possible, and frequent, that white tells darker than black; that is, if white on the underside falls into sharp shadow it is apt to be actually darker in value than black on the top, shining in or bathed in much light. These things must all be studied conscientiously and with a wide-open mind, as all our natural ideas are apt to be violated when actual conditions are studiously examined. The way to do is to take any subject you want—preferably in

White-breasted Nuthatch
Sitta carolinensis
Watercolor
14¼″ × 18″
New York, 1898

American Anhinga
Anhinga anhinga
Pencil study sketches
15″ × 11″

simple design and colors at first—and do a picture of it three or four times, in different lights and positions, to accustom yourself to its changes, and get away from your traditional prejudices that a given surface is always to be represented by the same pigment or in the same manner. In other words, *loosen up,* be unafraid to try and represent what you see. It won't hurt anything if it does turn out awful; it may turn out right, and in any case you've learned something, either to do or not to do. And that is progress, while plodding in the track of prejudice without courage to kick out and see what happens is not going to develop anything better than it has already developed.[18]

Because of the experimental nature of his work, Fuertes discarded most of his 1897–1898 Dublin and Scarborough studies soon after discussing them with Abbott Thayer. In the few paintings that do survive from this period there is a softer outline and an improved anatomical accuracy. Despite Coues' admonitions against distracting foliage and other "stage setting" for his illustrations for *Citizen Bird,* Fuertes continued to include suggestions of natural settings as important compositional elements. A splintered branch in his white-breasted nuthatch study of February 24, 1898, and the supporting

42

6

american anhinga - a Snake bird
Plotus anhinga

vegetation in several sparrow paintings made during the same winter provide structure for the pictures and suggest his continuing interest in concealing coloration. Although the birds and vegetation are depicted against a stark white ground, similar and complementary pigments are used for the birds and their settings. A delicate watercolor study of a junco in a flaming red fall sumac (probably from the same period) reflects another of Fuertes' interests: the subtleties of light and color within a superficially monochromatic subject. With its dark grey back and white breast, the slate-colored junco must have suggested to Fuertes the logical extremes of natural countershading principles.

In March 1898, after nine months of study with Thayer that brought him "immense pleasure and profit,"[19] Fuertes joined Abbott Thayer, Gerald Thayer, and a young artist named Charles Knight on a bird-collecting and painting trip in Florida. The trip resulted in much more than an impressive collection of study skins taken from northbound migrants in spring plumage. With its camaraderie, adventures, and opportunities for nature study, the six-week excursion was a memorable one for all involved. Fuertes found a lasting friend in Charles Knight who, like Fuertes, was experiencing his first scientific expedition. They shared in the excitement of exploring new habitats and in collecting the brilliant birds that fascinated them.

Fuertes' 1898 trip to Florida with Abbott Thayer included (l to r): LAF, Charles R. Knight, Alden H. Hadley, Gerald Thayer, and Abbott Thayer. This photograph was taken on St. John's Marshes west of Melbourne, Florida. A photograph of Fuertes from the same trip shows evidence of his shooting skill at the age of twenty-four.

At the close of the Florida trip, Charles Knight went to New York, the Thayers left for Europe, and Fuertes returned to his family in Ithaca. Through the fall and winter of 1898 he continued his intensive study of light, color, and ornithological anatomy.

A PAINTER OF LIFE

Fuertes' ability to put his birds in lifelike poses was one of his greatest strengths as an artist and, in Thayer's opinion, compensated for his inadequate treatment of colors. "You are extraordinary in the intimate way you represent [birds]," he wrote Fuertes, "and manage with impure values and color . . . nevertheless to unite in each picture so much revelation of the secrets of each bird's personal appearance as to mark genius on it."[20] A small watercolor study of a dead black-throated blue warbler inscribed "Kayutah Lake, Sept. 10 '98" suggests Thayer's influence on the developing artist. While its quality is consistent with other Fuertes studies of the period, its treatment of a dead specimen is atypical; it may have been an attempt to master the subtleties of color without the distraction of pose, and so rectify the "impurities" of which Thayer so often complained.

The Thayers' frequent depictions of dead subjects—and Fuertes' instinct for picturing them alive—is significant, for it reveals not only their different temperaments but also confirms Thayer's observation that "you are coming into bird-art through the bird end, like a bird, in fact, while Gerald approaches them through Art itself."[21] It was a difference Fuertes recognized and accepted. He saw no value in the painterly tradition of depicting dead game as still life. To Fuertes, bird skins were simply study tools, a means for creating vignettes of life.

Like Wilson and Audubon before him, Fuertes recognized the essential role of collected skins and field sketches from freshly killed specimens in ornithological portraiture. But unlike the Thayers, who were more interested in the visual interplay of plumage and light, Fuertes considered the details of feather color and anatomy only a part of the bigger picture. Frank Chapman's account of Fuertes' concentration in the field reveals the importance Fuertes gave to his subjects in both death and life—and the intensity with which he worked:

> Fuertes in possession of a freshly captured specimen of some bird which was before unknown to him is, for the time, wholly beyond the reach of all sensations other than those occasioned by the specimen before him. His concentration annihilates his surroundings. Color, pattern, form, contour, minute details of structure, all are absorbed and assimilated so completely that they become part of himself, and they can be reproduced at any future time with amazing accuracy. Less consciously, but not less thoroughly and effectively, does he store impressions of the bird's appearance in life, its pose, mannerisms, characteristic gestures of wings, tail or crest, its facial expression—all are recorded with surprising fidelity.[22]

Although Fuertes was as good a shot with a collecting pistol or shotgun as he had been with a slingshot in his youth, he did not kill birds for the sake of killing. As Chapman observed, once Fuertes had "acquired specimens adequately representing a bird's appearance, [he] experienced no further desire to collect it."[23] Wilfred Osgood, the zoologist who accompanied Fuertes on the Field Museum's Abyssinian Expedition of 1926–1927, observed a paradox in Fuertes' behavior toward the killing that was a necessary part of his profession: "With gun in hand he was a hunter and collector, having no qualms about the shedding of blood, but with a freshly killed bird before him he would sometimes sit stroking its feathers in a detached ecstasy, purring and crooning over it in a manner that in another might have seemed ridiculous."[24]

It is worth noting that, for all of the potentially violent subjects Fuertes painted during his lifetime, he rarely depicted violence in action. While his birds of prey often clutch small birds or mammals in their talons, they are almost never shown killing them. The violence is implied; the scene is usually tranquil. While this mood may sometimes be attributed to client preference, the nature of Fuertes' study sketches and other private drawings suggests that he chose to see harmony and balance in the world around him. A series of pencil sketches of a rabbit, made in the teens or twenties as preparation for a large bird-of-prey commission, provides some insight into his attitude toward death. The rabbit is drawn peacefully, as if in sleep. Instead of agony, there is repose.

Ironically, Fuertes drew conspicuous attention to the victims of his birds of prey in paintings commissioned by the Church and Dwight Company for reproduction on baking-soda cards. The company, which had already distributed Fuertes' songbird and game bird cards in its Arm and Hammer boxes, had doubts about the suitability of the bird-of-prey series for children, the most avid collectors of the cards, and declined to publish the paintings. A rediscovery of the originals in 1976 prompted Church and Dwight to print the cards more than fifty years after they were painted. Even then, most of the prey-bearing birds were omitted from the set.

Fuertes felt strongly about protecting birds of prey and contributed many of his paintings to the cause of public education by providing illustrations for United States Government publications and educational brochures at reduced rates. In his public lectures, he saluted birds for their part in controlling agricultural pests. He believed these birds were badly misunderstood and unjustifiably maligned. This may have been another reason why he understated the violence of the larger bird predators or often selected "pest" mammals for their victims.

He felt differently about insect eaters. When Fuertes painted sparrow hawks, he usually showed them devouring their prey (grasshoppers), something he would seldom have considered for a mammal-eating bird. Another example of his calling attention to the concept of selective prey is a water-

46

Dead Rabbit studies, Pencil, 14½″ × 12″

American Kestrel, *Falco sparverius*, Watercolor, 12″ × 9″

color he prepared for an Agriculture Department bulletin in 1914. It shows a Brewer's blackbird consuming a large alfalfa weevil, while in the background a farmer plows his field, followed by a hungry flock of the same species. Here, the predator consuming an agricultural pest is emphasized to complement the text and rectify a misunderstanding about the habits—and usefulness—of the bird depicted. The painting and the pamphlet it illustrated were intended to convince farmers that the Brewer's blackbird was actually an aid to agriculture, consuming weevils, not seeds, as it flocked behind the plow.

Fuertes returned to the Thayers' in the winter of 1898–1899, encouraged by news that Abbott and Gerald had collected a large number of bird specimens while in Europe. Thayer was eager to have Fuertes stay with the family, having written several times from abroad imploring him to come to Scarborough. He promised to be "still more deferential" to Fuertes' desire to paint birds instead of plaster casts. "I now believe in your doing just birds," he wrote from Italy. "You are too peculiar to need or profit by academic training."[25]

It had become clear to Thayer that birds were at the root of Fuertes' interest in art and that nothing he could do or say would alter that single

Brewer's Blackbird
Euphagus cyanocephalus
Watercolor
11″ × 15″
c. 1914

49

overriding focus. He resigned himself to "polishing the diamond"[26] he saw in Fuertes, without trying to recut its facets.

In January 1899, Elliott Coues sent Fuertes news of an exciting new commission: the illustration of a reissued edition of his *Key to North American Birds*. The job offered not only income ($20 per picture), but also the chance for increased recognition. "Besides the cash payments," wrote Coues, "I shall of course be glad to give you all possible credit in the preface of the book—or even, if you make pictures enough to warrant it, I may be able to place your name on the title page of the *Key* with my own."[27]

Fuertes was delighted by the commission and began at once to produce the dozens of bird-head vignettes required for the project. Working in black-and-white wash to ensure accurate reproduction, he captured so much of the

Great Horned Owl
Bubo virginianus
Pencil study, 7″ × .4″

Watercolor, 24″ × 16″
(at right)

essential characteristics of build, feather pattern, and attitude in each head that depicting an entire body was unnecessary. Fuertes' ability to distill identifying features in his subjects—first revealed in the plates for *Citizen Bird* and *A-Birding on a Bronco,* and carried further in the illustrations for Coues' *Key*—established him as the preeminent ornithological illustrator of his time.

Fuertes' work for Coues was interrupted in the spring of 1899 by the invitation to join Edward Henry Harriman and his party on the expedition to Alaska. The two-month trip (described in detail in Part III) was a tremendous experience for Fuertes, affording an opportunity to see large reaches of little-known terrain, to collect and draw hundreds of new bird species, and to meet and work with some of the most influential scientists of the period. Coues wrote Fuertes just before his departure, urging him to "use your time to the best possible purpose in your art" and to return "with very full portfolios of all sorts of interesting things, as well as in perfect health, ready to resume and push to completion the important business you have on hand with my publisher and myself."[28] Fuertes did all of these things, satisfying in the process his love of travel and adventure. The sketches he made on the trip would serve as valuable references for Coues' *Key* and for many other commissions in the years to come. Sixteen were adapted for color reproduction in Harriman's expedition reports (published jointly by the Washington Academy of Sciences and the Smithsonian Institution).

THE FUERTES STYLE

In the year-and-a-half between his trip to Alaska and his next major expedition—to Texas in the summer of 1901—Fuertes noticeably improved his painting style. The meticulous detail and sometimes faulty anatomy of his earlier work gave way to a bolder, more painterly, and more consistently accurate treatment of his subject matter. No longer did he use the formal, Audubonesque poses and stylized foliage treatment of his college days. With increased field experience and a growing self-confidence, he created spontaneous, lifelike compositions of real birds in specific locations. Fuertes continued to draw inspiration from Audubon, but his work now had its own distinctive style.

It is hard to pinpoint a single cause for Fuertes' development between his Alaskan trip and 1901. No doubt, Abbott Thayer's instruction and the success of his commercial ventures had much to do with this artistic maturation. It is also conceivable that Elliott Coues' death on December 25, 1899, changed Fuertes' own image of himself. No longer the discovered, youthful, dependent student, he was now clearly his own man, with a reputation based on accomplishment and not merely promise.

As if to announce this important artistic and personal transition, Fuertes gave up the angular "LAF" with which he had signed his work since first

52

Three Sparrow heads
Ink wash
5″ × 5½″ each

sending it to Coues for criticism in 1895. In 1900, he began to use rounded letters and, composition permitting, signed his name in full. With a new signature and a new painting style, Louis Agassiz Fuertes welcomed the new century. At the age of twenty-six, his career was already in full stride.

Orders were now coming to Fuertes at a tremendous rate. Some of the larger commissions in the first few years of the decade included illustrations for *Birdcraft* by Mabel Osgood Wright (1900); *The Second Book of Birds* by Olive Thorne Miller (1901); *The Woodpeckers* by Fannie Hardy Eckstorm (1901); *Upland Game Birds* by Edwyn Sandys and T.S. Van Dyke (1902); *Birds of the Rockies* by Leander S. Keyser (1902); *Handbook of Birds of the Western United States* by Florence Merriam Bailey (1902), and *The Economic Value of Birds to the State* [*of New York*] by Frank M. Chapman (1902). Chapman's book, published by the State of New York, represents the beginning of a long and fruitful association between Fuertes and the state's Forest, Fish, and Game Commission, culminating in 1910 with the publication of a

53

Common Goldeneye, *Bucephala clangula*, Ink wash, 9¼″ × 7½″. The rounded initials date the painting at left after 1900. Common Goldeneye, *Bucephala clangula*, Ink wash, 5¾″ × 7″. The angular initials date the painting of the same species at right prior to 1900.

Yellow–bellied Sapsucker,
Sphyrapicus varius varius
Red–naped Sapsucker,
Sphyrapicus varius nuchalis
Red–breasted Sapsucker,
Sphyrapicus varius daggetti
Watercolor
18″ × 12″

comprehensive two–volume work on the *Birds of New York*. It was written
by Elon Howard Eaton and had more than a hundred color plates by Fuertes.
The earlier state publication was also among the first of a lifelong series of
cooperative ventures between Fuertes and Chapman.

The two men had known each other ever since Fuertes attended his first
AOU congress in 1896. They admired each other's work, took an instant
liking to each other, and enjoyed each other's company at home and in the

field for the next thirty years. Beginning in 1904, Chapman regularly included color plates by Fuertes in his influential magazine *Bird-Lore*. He also employed him to assist in preparing several large habitat groups constructed in the bird hall of the American Museum of Natural History in New York.

Like Coues, whose position as the country's leading ornithologist he soon filled, Chapman recognized Fuertes' outstanding abilities as an artist. Unlike Coues, he encouraged Fuertes to incorporate backgrounds and other references to environmental habitat in his bird paintings. Although not as daring as Abbott Thayer, who later urged Fuertes to make his birds invisible against a natural setting, Chapman did not believe in the austerity of composition required by Coues. In a letter discussing the New York Forest, Fish, and Game Commission plates of 1902, he struck the middle ground, reinforcing Fuertes' own instinct for compromise: "My own preference in the matter of background is for what you term 'a dash of environment;' at any rate a suggestion of haunt, something more than a silhouette against a clean white background."[29]

Fuertes successfully developed the "dash of environment" formula that would become a hallmark of his commercial painting around the turn of the

Harlequin Quail
(Merriam's Quail)
Cyrtonyx montezumae
Watercolor study with
White-throated Jay, 9¼″ × 12″

Merriam's Quail.

Mexican birds.

Recently described Jay.

Harlequin Quail, *Cyrtonyx montezumae*, Watercolor, 11¼″ × 9″, 1903

Horned and
Tufted Puffins
Fratercula corniculata
and *Lunda cirrhata*
Wash on grey paper
13″ × 8½″

To Harry L. Ferguson
travelling Sept 17, 1923 - at Fisher's Island.

Erolia ferruginea

century, when so many other stylistic changes appeared in his work. While most of Fuertes' 1899 Alaska paintings were of individual birds against a white ground or stylized suggestions of branches and leaves in the Audubon tradition, one painting made to illustrate the Harriman expedition report the year after his return represents an important change in the artist's approach to setting.

It is an ink wash on grey paper of a group of horned and tufted puffins on a rocky ledge, surrounded by individual studies of other puffins in flight and on the water. In the central vignette of the preliminary study and the final published work (to which an extra puffin was added), Fuertes skillfully integrated the birds and their habitat. The grassy boulders of the cliff are treated not as decorative embellishments to a series of isolated puffin studies, but as an essential part of the overall composition. The simple but effective approach employed in this puffin group is one he would continue to develop in Texas during the summer of 1901.

Fuertes had been receiving painting assignments from the Division of Economic Ornithology and Mammalogy of the Department of Agriculture ever since its dynamic leader, C. Hart Merriam, saw his work at the 1896

Curlew Sandpiper
Calidris ferruginea
Watercolor
11″ × 15″
New York, 1923

Roadrunner
Geococcyx californianus
Ink study (left), 8½″ × 11″
Ink wash (below), 11″ × 14″

Watercolor (head), 9″ × 11½″
Texas, 1901 (at right)

Louis Agassiz Fuertes.

San Antonio –
April 14, 1901

AOU congress. It was Merriam who had suggested that Fuertes be invited on the Harriman Alaska Expedition, and it was again Merriam who arranged for Fuertes' participation in the government-sponsored study in 1901.

In his "Results of a Biological Survey of the San Francisco Mountain Region and Desert of the Little Colorado in Arizona," published in the Agriculture Department's *North American Fauna* (1890), Merriam first developed the theory of "life zones" based on different climatic conditions rather than arbitrary geo-political boundaries. Using this approach, Merriam's Division of Economic Ornithology and Mammalogy—later the Bureau of Biological Survey—set out systematically to examine the flora and fauna of North America. The biological survey of Texas, whose staff included Fuertes, was one of a series that inventoried plant and animal life from Death Valley (1891) to Hudson's Bay (1900) and from Alaska (1903 and 1904) to Wyoming (1909–1916).

The Texas experience was exhilarating to Fuertes, and although working conditions were frequently miserable, he was able to study a wider variety of birds than on any previous trip. Fuertes' charge was to paint as many of the region's birds as he could observe and capture. He produced hundreds of paintings—purchased by the government at rates of $20 to $30 each—that reflect his growing confidence and competence as a painter.

Always a hard worker in the field, Fuertes made the most of every opportunity. Just one day after his arrival in San Antonio at the start of the trip, he made a series of small field sketches and a color head study of a roadrunner.

61

Together, they provide a record of his working methods and an example of his ability to capture the essence of a bird after only a short period of observation. In a letter of a few days later, the artist described his subject:

> . . . I have made two or three colored studies—one of a queer snub-nosed cardinal and another of a road-runner's head. This last is *the* freak bird out here, and that is saying a lot. He has a wonderful patch of painted skin from around his eye clear to the back of his head. It is covered by overlapping feathers most of the time—but when he cocks his tail and throws up his top-knot he peals a place as big as a peanut on each side of his pate that is white and blue and vivid deep orange!![30]

Fuertes started his Texan sojourn alone in San Antonio and Comstock. By the time he met ornithologist Harry C. Oberholser in Langtry almost two weeks later, he had already collected seventy-five different bird specimens. A

Long-eared Owl
Asio otus
Pencil study, 13½″ × 9½″

Watercolor, 14″ × 11″
(at right)

perennial enthusiast, Fuertes was at first resentful of Oberholser's "knowall calmness over everything" and preferred to work alone "where at least I have no damper to my gloat."[31] But after the two joined Vernon Bailey, chief field naturalist of the Biological Survey and technical leader of the expedition, personal relations improved. "The party gets on fine together," he wrote from Tornillo Creek on May 23rd, "and we have bully talks o'nights or jogging along on our ponies through this great country."[32]

Bailey, whose collecting interests differed from those of the two ornithologists, focused his attention on mammals, insects, reptiles, and amphibians, frequently bringing his prize specimens to Fuertes. Among the subjects other than birds painted by Fuertes during the trip are a number of mam-

63

mals, a whip scorpion or vinegarroon, and several lizards, one of which was captured for him by Bailey near the Rio Grande:

> We broke camp early next day and travelled all day thro' marvellous desert mountain country with curious lizards sprinting away ahead of us, or snuggling up along some stone or stick. Some of these lizards go beyond anything I ever imagined for beauty, agility and general attractiveness. They are mostly small, but some get quite decent in size. I spent nearly all yesterday afternoon painting pictures of a glorious little translucent creature called *callosaurus,* which Bailey had caught alive for me to look at and I painted him alive. It was great sport, but exceedingly difficult as he is made up of a whole set of high bright colors put on in little round spots.[33]

Nor were Fuertes' interests in Texas limited to wildlife. He became fascinated by the area's Indian culture. "The thing that gives the places their greatest interest," he wrote, "is the evidence all about of a long dead human

Greater Earless Lizard
Holbrookia texana
Wash, 7″ × 7¼″
Texas, 1901

Great Curassow, *Crax rubra*, Watercolor, 15″ × 11″

Sharp-shinned Hawk
Accipiter striatus
Watercolor
11 ½″ × 7¼″

occupancy."[34] The bold geometric designs he found on the walls of caves, like those in the baskets and blankets he purchased from the living Indians there, inspired some of his later work, including border designs for bookplates created for friends and acquaintances well into the 1920s.

As Abbott Thayer observed in 1897, Louis Agassiz Fuertes was a talented artist who never moved in "art circles."[35] In the thousands of letters he wrote to friends, family, and colleagues, he frequently described plants, animals, landscapes, and situations, but never mentioned visiting an art museum or admiring the work of another artist not involved with wildlife art. And yet, in some of his paintings there are similarities to other painting styles or movements that are hard to attribute to coincidence alone. Most notable of these is a series of black-and-white washes with a decidedly oriental flavor, which he began to produce shortly after his return from Texas.

Preliminary sketches for one such painting, of a sora, indicate that Fuertes settled on the foreshortened pose and uplifted foot used in the final composition only after experimenting with a range of other possibilities. The sketches may represent his field observations, but no specific date or location is marked on them. They are probably studio sketches, in which the artist called on his memory to create a pleasing composition that would accurately reflect the bird's appearance and behavior. His final selection combines the pose of the head and body in one drawing with the treatment of the foot in another. It captures the wary hesitation of this wetland bird and successfully transforms a potentially awkward subject into a graceful one. The delicate treatment of the middle- and background sedges and the watery reflections they impart completes the composition with understated elegance.

Similar paintings of wading birds from the same period convey a sufficiently Eastern flavor to be grouped with the sora as reflecting an oriental style in Fuertes' oeuvre. Excellent examples are an American bittern now in the Cornell University Collection and a pair of green herons at The Academy of Natural Sciences in Philadelphia.

What may have sparked the style is not entirely clear. Although Fuertes' interest in oriental art is confirmed by his fondness for a large Japanese wall hanging given him by a friend from architecture school, there is no evidence of any direct exposure to Japanese or Chinese painting at the time when his work seemed most influenced by oriental art. He may have developed the style independently or drawn inspiration from prints or paintings encountered through Abbott Thayer and in his domestic travels. The source may never be known.

Charles Livingston Bull, an illustrator contemporary with Fuertes, capitalized on the public's fondness for oriental design in his wildlife paintings. He achieved popular and financial success through magazine commissions, but never received the acclaim of the scientific community enjoyed by

67

Sora
Porzana carolina
Pencil sketches

Ink wash, 15″ × 9¾″
(at right)

Louis Agassiz Fuertes.

Fuertes. Bull's work—strong, evocative, and stylized—was ideally suited to the growing number of animal stories appearing in books and magazines at the time. But this was not the kind of work Fuertes enjoyed. While he agreed to undertake a number of popular magazine commissions, he preferred the more exacting requirements of his scientific colleagues. They, in turn, preferred accuracy to ambiance, and Fuertes, recognizing his own strengths in this area, was willing to oblige.

Even with his self-imposed limitations of subject, Fuertes was frequently offered more commissions than he could fill. Publishers persisted, as is evident, for example, in Fuertes' 1901 correspondence with Caspar Whitney, president and editor of the Outing Publishing Company. When Whitney had asked Fuertes for illustrations of game cocks to accompany an article in *Outing* magazine, the artist was hard at work on a $1,050 contract with Houghton Mifflin to produce thirty-three plates for Florence Merriam Bailey's *Handbook of Birds of the Western United States.* He declined Whitney's invitation, explaining that he had a great deal of work on hand and was about to embark on a five-month biological survey of Texas. "I am very sorry to hear that you can't do the game cocks right away," replied Whitney, "but tell me when you can do them and I will wait for you."[36]

A NEW DEPARTURE

In the summer of 1915, Louis Fuertes made a bold departure from his well-established and successful career in bird painting. Gilbert Grosvenor asked Fuertes to produce a series of plates on "The Larger North American Mammals" for *National Geographic Magazine,* and Fuertes accepted the commission, which followed the publication of three successful issues featuring color reproductions of Fuertes' birds (June 1913, May 1914, and August 1915). It proved a much more difficult and time-consuming assignment than any Fuertes had previously attempted.

Fuertes was about to plunge into untested waters. His previous depiction of mammals had been limited to the small prey shown as victims of his hawks and owls, and a few life studies for Vernon Bailey and the Department of Agriculture. For the next three years he would spend the greatest part of his time familiarizing himself with the appearance and behavior of animals with which he had little direct experience.

His numerous mammal plates for "The Larger North American Mammals" (November 1916), "The Smaller North American Mammals" (May 1918), and "Our Common Dogs" (March 1919) were enthusiastically received by Grosvenor and the public, but Fuertes questioned their quality. He also found them extremely taxing to produce. "I've done the best I could under the circumstances," he wrote Joseph Grinnell, director of the Museum

Green Heron, *Butorides virescens*, Wash, 12″ × 9½″

of Vertebrate Zoology at the University of California. "You can readily believe it was a matter of considerable study for me, who have never particularly specialized on mammals and I am very anxious for the verdict. It was only undertaken because the need seemed so great and the opportunity so good."[37]

The "need" was probably Fuertes' own, for during the troubled war years he found it difficult to support his growing family (he and his wife Madge now had two children) on steadily decreasing commissions. The need could not have been for Fuertes the painter, for he knew several well-qualified mammal painters who could have undertaken the assignment. His long-time friend Charles Knight and Carl Rungius were two painters he particularly admired. In a letter of a few years later, Fuertes praised their ability to depict mammals and tried to explain to an aspiring artist the value of familiarity

Blacktail Jackrabbit
Lepus californicus
Ink wash study, 9″ × 7½″

Ink wash, 14″ × 11″
(at right)

L. A. Fuertes.

with one's subject. In so doing, he suggests the difficulties he himself faced in completing the commission:

> It is hard I know to do good drawing at the Zoo. I've been through it and I may say that I never did well at it. But in animal and bird drawing there is no alternative. You must be a clean draughtsman and nothing in the world but faithful work and lots of it will ever make you one. . . . Men like Knight and Rungius develop a wonderful sense of animals that transcends their knowledge of anatomy and enables them to express character to a degree that seems almost uncanny. But there is no miracle about it. They are simply excellent draughtsmen who have worked without stint and in so doing have so familiarized themselves with their subjects that the ordinary difficulties have entirely disappeared. And the labor can all be turned into the ultimate interpretation of those things which to the less ardent student seem the mysterious insight denied them. I personally think that there is no mystery to it after granting right off that the study required is impossible to one not possessing the sympathy and interest in sufficient degree to hold them to the job through the discouragements of the long beginnings.[38]

Fuertes did not have familiarity with mammals, and his efforts to achieve it left him discouraged and exhausted. "I don't believe I'll allow myself again to be seriously diverted from my real work, for which I've concentrated everything all these years," he wrote Frank Chapman in the spring of 1918:

> Never before has a winter's work been so strenuous as that of the past eight months because for the greater part, I suppose, it has been in a field absolutely untried, requiring a vast amount of study and preparation which in my regular work has been spread out over the many years that you and I have worked side by side. The result is that it has left me more tired and with a greater repugnance for brushes and paints than I have ever in my life experienced. I am not very temperamental as a rule, but I certainly have soured on paint. . . .[39]

Some of the discouragement reflected in Fuertes' letter may have come from Abbott and Gerald Thayer's negative reaction to his *National Geographic* series.

The Thayers may have wished more evidence of concealing coloration in Fuertes' work, but Gilbert Grosvenor and Fuertes' other publishers were well satisfied by the artist's compromise between subject and setting. In the summer of 1918, Grosvenor gloated over the success of Fuertes' mammal series and tried to interest him in yet another new subject area. He was convinced that Fuertes could accomplish anything he put his mind to:

> The Geographic has done many fine things, but none really more beneficial for mankind than our persuading the genius Fuertes to enter the field of animal painting. Your first Mammals was good, your Smaller Mammals was better, and now your Dogs are the best of all. I have just been looking over the entire 32 plates, and I believe for variety, beauty, animation and interest they are unsurpassed and will make as much of a sensation as everything else that you have done. The Dogs have been the very hardest kind of work and often distasteful, but when you look back on the months devoted to the series I hope you will feel the job was not such a bad one after all.

St. Bernard, *Canis familiaris inostranzewi,* Watercolor, 16″ × 13″

Ringtail
Bassariscus astutus
Watercolor
16″ × 13″

I wish you could tackle the heavens next. I would give anything if we could find somebody to depict the stars in a picturesque and intelligent way. Do you think you could tackle the job?![40]

Fuertes replied that he was "the standard of ignorance" on stars and felt "entirely inadequate to even consider such an undertaking,"[41] and confided in Frank Chapman that "I thought there were a few things on earth we hadn't tried."[42]

By this time, Grosvenor was eager for anything Fuertes would paint. He wrote again suggesting a series on fishes, reptiles, or butterflies, but Fuertes wanted to return to his favorite subject. After considerable research, he prepared text and illustrations for an article on the history of falconry entitled "Falconry, the Sport of Kings" and a companion piece on "American Birds of Prey—A Review of Their Value." Both articles were published in *National Geographic* in December 1920.

It is significant that for his own bookplate, Fuertes selected the peregrine falcon, long admired as the fastest and most agile of the world's avian predators and a subject he never tired of painting. "I believe you know that the birds of prey are little less than a passion with me," he wrote to a colleague in 1915.[43] It was a passion he reflected in his art. Though he sometimes tired of other subjects, he relished commissions for birds of prey. "They are to me what the big cats are to Knighty," he once wrote, referring to Charles Knight, whose paintings of feline predators he particularly admired.[44]

Five Loons (Red-throated, *Gavia stellata*; Common, *Gavia immer*; and Arctic, *Gavia arctica*). A preliminary study of a plate for *Birds of New York* by Elon H. Eaton (1910). Watercolor, 5¼" × 8¾", New York, 1907.

Fuertes did not limit his interest in birds of prey to the studio. When he could speak out in their defense, he did so knowledgeably and with conviction. When the superintendent of a state game farm in Minnesota issued a public call to exterminate several hawk and owl species, Fuertes wrote:

Dear Sir:—

I have just recd. and read the Jan. number of 'American Game'—and my attention was arrested by your report on vermin control. I have had enough experience and knowledge of this matter to know that it is serious, but I cannot refrain from voicing my strong disapproval and urging that you go at this with a more tolerant mind, for many of the species listed as vermin and indiscriminately killed certainly do not belong there, and I think you would have a hard time showing an unbiased balance against nearly a third of your list. . . . It is stupid in the extreme to condemn everything that comes around the game farm on suspicion, and you would have the farmers in arms against you if they knew the value, to them, of such of your victims as the broadwing, sparrowhawk, long- and short-eared owls, barn owl, rough-leg hawk, and all the little owls, for you are thereby removing the control from *real* vermin—rats & field-mice chiefly, & grasshoppers and harmful insects, that really cost the farmer hard money. . . .[45]

Whether or not Fuertes' authority on bird behavior was acknowledged by government officials, it was usually accepted by ornithologists. If the pose or attitude of a familiar bird was challenged by a client, Fuertes could invariably support the accuracy of his depiction with his own field observations. When Frank Chapman expressed doubts about the leg position of a sharp-shinned hawk shown carrying its prey in flight, for example, Fuertes replied with a characteristically thorough defense of his painting:

The hawk is all right. I have watched practically all genera shown, and all do as I've shown *accipiter*: carry the prey at almost leg-length, and slightly back. Sparrow-hawks carry mice that way. Ospreys invariably carry fish (vide Abbott). Roughlegs carry even small field mice that way, and peregrines, doves. This I am as sure of as that they use their wings in flying, and have repeatedly observed it. In all the cases I have ever seen of a hawk or eagle carrying prey it has always been carried well away from the body. They have no instinct to bring their feet forward in flight, as they carry them stowed under the u. tail coverts and extended. I think only *passeres* carry their feet forward in the belly feathers in flight. There may be others, but not *raptores*.[46]

Subsequent high-speed photographs, unavailable in Fuertes' time, confirm that his observations and depictions were completely accurate.

"Your little blue heron experience is almost as amusing as it is exasperating," he wrote to his friend, the artist Allan Brooks, after Brooks described criticism he received for the colors of a bird he had drawn from life.

I've *so* many times had the same or similar brushes with those in high places, matching definite first-hand knowledge with long-standing notions. Nobody not visual-minded can possibly know how much gets by unobserved and unnoted by those even whose business it should be to 'discern' and record the

A composition of owl heads, Wash, 13¼″ × 17″, 1912

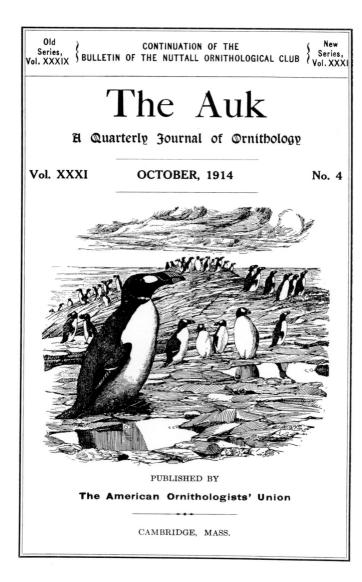

Old Series, Vol. XXXIX } CONTINUATION OF THE BULLETIN OF THE NUTTALL ORNITHOLOGICAL CLUB { New Series, Vol. XXXI

The Auk

A Quarterly Journal of Ornithology

Vol. XXXI   **OCTOBER, 1914**   **No. 4**

PUBLISHED BY

The American Ornithologists' Union

CAMBRIDGE, MASS.

Cover for *The Auk,* 1914, showing Fuertes' first design.

common things—much more the difficult or rarely encountered ones. Any bird or animal painter knows, with anguish often, what a stubborn and exasperating thing prejudice or preconception can be.[47]

Unfortunately, Fuertes could not always work from live specimens. In plates for unfamiliar birds, he was dependent on written descriptions and study skins that he borrowed in person or by mail from the American Museum of Natural History, The Academy of Natural Sciences, or elsewhere. Sometimes, as in his *Great Curassow,* Fuertes referred to landscape photographs in order to insure the accuracy of backgrounds for birds he had not been able to observe in the field. Ironically, a commission that caused a great flurry of criticism was that of an extinct species.

Asked in 1912 to design a new cover for the American Ornithologists'

Cover for *The Auk,* 1915, showing Fuertes' second and final design.

Old Series, Vol. XL

CONTINUATION OF THE
BULLETIN OF THE NUTTALL ORNITHOLOGICAL CLUB

New Series, Vol. XXXII

The Auk

A Quarterly Journal of Ornithology

Vol. XXXII   JANUARY, 1915   No. 1

PUBLISHED BY

The American Ornithologists' Union

CAMBRIDGE, MASS.

Union's prestigious journal, *The Auk,* Fuertes' challenge was to improve on an anatomically inaccurate version of the extinct bird that had appeared on the publication's cover since 1884. Basing his initial sketch on a mounted specimen, skeletal measurements, and photographs of Funk Island, where the auks once lived, he submitted his drawings to Drs. Chapman, Elliott, and Lucas of the AOU. Their suggestions for improvement ranged from head to toe and even included the pose of background birds: "The second largest bird in the background, which is waving its wings, introduces a debatable question as to the position of the wings, and we think it would be desirable to have the wings close to the body to avoid any ground for argument. . . . it is essential that [the drawing] be above criticism. ∴ ."[48] Dutifully incorporating their recommendations in the final design, Fuertes

81

mailed the drawing to AOU council member and *Auk* editor, Witmer Stone, in Philadelphia. The poem with which he accompanied it is typical of Fuertes' good humor.

> The locus of this bird defunct
>   (Where Lucas and his comrades bunked)
> Is on the Island known as Funk
>   Where awkward Auks lived, died and stunk.
>
> The picture shows perhaps a score
>   (Tho' there were doubtless many more)
> A settin on the very stones
>   Where Lucas gang got all their bones.
>
> A wise committee in New York
>   Have passed their word that this 'ere Auk
> Conforms in feature and proportion
>   To the Museum's stuffed abortion.
>
> As to position, wings and such
>   The critics don't know very much
> So I just guessed my very best
>   Imagination did the rest.
>
> *L'Envoi*
>
> And this we have for comfort sweet
>   Should doctors disagree
> Nobody lives who knew the beast
>   And there are no more to see.
>
> So if they do not like its looks
>   What can they do about it?
> Our guess is just as good as theirs
>   So if they scoff we'll scout it![49]

Stone replied with a rhyme of his own:

My dear Fuertes:

Your admirable Auk sketch has just come to hand this afternoon and *The Auk* sends thanks and congratulations:

> Twelve months ago, as you may know
> The Auk regained its flight
> And travelled 90 miles or so
> All in a single night.
>
> From Gotham, where its perch had been
> And where it gained renown
> It flew south to the Delaware
> Where Penn had built a town.
>
> And wise men said, 'This cannot be;
> This can't be that same Auk
> That lived content for 30 years
> With J.A.A., New Yauk.'

82

Peregrine Falcon, *Falco peregrinus*, Watercolor, 28½″ × 21¼″, 1913

Elk
Cervus canadensis
Watercolor
11″ × 22½″

And lo! we see they were correct
A new Auk had been hatched
He's much less goose-like than of yore.
For grace he's hard to match.

'Whence came this bird: Did Col. Thayer
Set his eggs to a hen?'
'No! Such fine birds have but one source'
Fuertes with his pen!

Merry X-mas and all good wishes

Sincerely yours
Witmer Stone[50]

Despite the exhaustive research that had gone into it, no sooner had the drawing appeared in print than it was criticized. None of the AOU members had ever seen the bird in life, but each "knew" how it should look! In November 1914, Witmer Stone described the situation in humorous iambic tetrameter:

The Muse, alas! has played us false
Our rhymes were all in vain
The Auk we praised has been condemned
We're forced to try again!

We thought that since the bird's extinct
Few critics there would be.
Alack! The Auk Authorities
Approach infinity![51]

Fortunately, Fuertes' final attempt at the cover design incorporated enough of the suggested improvements to be acceptable to everyone. It appeared in the 1915 issue and has been used by *The Auk* ever since.

Although Fuertes felt most at home depicting his chosen subjects in two dimensions—whether in pen and ink, watercolor, or, more rarely, oils—he was intrigued by the three-dimensionality of sculpture. He greatly admired the work of his friend Charles Knight, of James Lippit Clark, and of other members of the exhibition staff of the American Museum of Natural History.

At first, he used sculpture as an aid in his two-dimensional commissions.

Passenger Pigeon
Ectopistes migratorius
(extinct since 1914)
Ink wash
9½″ × 5½″

Lammergeier
Gypaetus barbatus
Watercolor study
10¾″ × 12¾″
Abyssinia, 1926

As he explained in a letter to Gilbert Grosvenor in 1918, he sometimes made small models of the animals he wished to draw:

> I can of course produce pictures of dogs, more or less formal and with little imagination as to action and settings, in shorter time than it would take to work out careful plans and spontaneous action. As you know, all dog fanciers (the only people that have their dogs photographed) have simple profiles taken to show "points"—regardless of the real beauty and naturalness of an unself-conscious dog. These are about the only available pictures. To translate these into action and informality means to model them in wax or clay and then "set them going" and draw them from the models. This takes not only great labor, but lots of time.[52]

Some nine years later, Fuertes created a more finished sculpture: a seated mountain gorilla with a butterfly on its hand. The original clay model, based on careful study of photographs, specimens, and live zoo models over a long period of time, was cast in bronze in 1923 and exhibited at the Pennsylvania Academy of the Fine Arts in 1925.[53] Its showing in the Academy's annual exhibition prompted favorable reviews in a number of French art journals.

Lammergeier
Gypaetus barbatus
Pencil field studies
10¾″ × 12⅝″
Abyssinia, 1926

Fuertes with Lammergeier
Arusi, Mt. Albasso,
Abyssinia, 1926

Common Crane, *Grus grus*, Watercolor study, 15¾" × 11⅞", Abyssinia, 1927

Dian Fossey, an authority on gorilla behavior, has recently noted that the sympathetic and sensitive depiction of the seated animal was well ahead of its time in conveying the peaceful nature of the species, which then was popularly believed to be quite ferocious. Fuertes' extensive research for the piece and his decision to cast and publicly exhibit it indicates his own confidence in the sculpture as a work of art. A somewhat less successful clay sculpture of an elk was cast in plaster in 1926, but it was never exhibited.

The limited extent of Fuertes' experimentation with sculpture may have been due, at least in part, to the heavy load of painting commissions he carried throughout his career. The twenties were an especially busy time for him professionally, for with the close of the war came a renewed surge of interest in and support for the natural sciences. In 1922 Fuertes entered into a long-term contract with ornithologist Edward Howe Forbush and the State of Massachusetts to provide plates for the *Birds of Massachusetts and Other New England States,* a massive undertaking that would take Forbush seven years to complete. At the same time, Fuertes produced illustrations for three important ornithological monographs: William Beebe's *Monograph of the Pheasants* (1922), John C. Phillips' *A Natural History of Ducks* (1922), and T. Gilbert Pearson's *Herons of the United States* (1924). In addition to these scientific commissions, Fuertes produced a commercial series of ninety bird portraits for Church and Dwight (Arm and Hammer Baking Soda) as described in Part I. Though lucrative and popular, these were certainly not Fuertes' finest works. In a letter to Wilfred Osgood, curator of zoology at the Field Museum, he once described them as "hum-drums and banalities."[54]

Two children's books he illustrated during this same period, *The [Thornton] Burgess Bird Book for Children* (1919) and *The Burgess Animal Book for Children* (1920), proved more interesting to him. Both received wide popular acclaim and sold extremely well. The *Animal Book* alone sold over 28,000 copies in the month-and-a-half following its publication.

Mountain Gorilla sculpture
as seen in its original clay model
before casting in 1923.

THE LATER YEARS

Fuertes, long recognized and admired by ornithologists, was fast becoming a national celebrity. He traveled back and forth across the country speaking before local Audubon groups, nature clubs, and conservation societies on a wide range of topics. "A Naturalist Among the Mayan Ruins of Yucatan," "Coloration of Animals: The Basis for the Science of Camouflage," and "Songs and Calls of Familiar Birds" were three of his most popular lectures. The last was perhaps his favorite, for his skills at song imitation were prodigious. In a letter of 1921, he described an upcoming trip to speak in Chicago, Cleveland, and Pittsburg, "where I severally sing, squeak, squawk, beller and hoot like Mother Nate-yure's little creat-yures. . . ."[55] Clearly, he enjoyed the opportunity to share his love of nature with a receptive public.

Beginning in 1922, the artist's long unofficial affiliation with the Cornell faculty was formalized by Livingston Farrand, president of the university. As "resident lecturer" at the university, Fuertes offered a yearly series of illustrated talks ranging in topic from zoological art and nature writing to bird migration, flight, coloration, and song. Arthur Allen, who would himself one day direct Cornell's ornithological program, attended many of Fuertes' lectures and described them in a 1927 issue of *Bird-Lore:*

> Fuertes was not an orator—his manner of speaking and frequent digressions often made it difficult for students to take notes on his lectures—but so vivid was his personality, so original his vocabulary, so humorous his metaphors and so warm his human sympathy, that notes were never necessary. Students left the classroom inspired. They remembered everything he said and discussed it among themselves as though it had been a baseball game.[56]

With all of his other activities and the seemingly endless string of visitors passing through his studio near campus, it is a wonder Fuertes was able to produce so much. Yet, during the late teens and early twenties, he not only continued his commissioned work, but also produced some of his finest private paintings. Selecting subjects for which he had special affection—such as hawks, owls, and falcons—Fuertes enjoyed the freedom of composing without the constraints of a publisher or the demands of a pressing client. He often adopted an especially large format in order to show off the birds and to include background details not required in his illustration commissions. These large watercolors, some of them his greatest works, were given or sold directly to friends, or sent to the prestigious Kennedy Galleries in New York, where they sold more quickly than he could paint them at prices of five to ten times that of his commissioned illustrations.

Fuertes' work load was so great by 1923 that he declined a tempting invitation to join an American Museum of Natural History research trip to Peru. "I have so much to do—and so much I've *had* to do is yet undone," he explained, summarizing his disappointment with a succinct, atypical "Hell!"[57]

When an even more tempting invitation came just three years later, the quest for new birds got the better of him. Temporarily shelving his *Birds of*

Snow Goose, *Chen hyperborea*, and Ring-necked Pheasant, *Phasianus colchicus,*
Watercolor and pencil study, 14″ × 10″

Massachusetts commission, he eagerly signed on to the Chicago Field Museum's Abyssinian Expedition, discussed more fully in Part III. "I look forward to the most thrilling as well as the most productive expedition of my whole experience," he wrote Stanley Field, president of the Field Museum.[58] In every sense, his expectations were realized.

The Field Museum agreed to pay Fuertes traveling expenses and $300 a month. In return, he would collect birds for the museum with the option of later obtaining duplicate specimens in exchange for other birds of his own. Any paintings or sketches he might make would be his personal property, with the understanding that he would lend them to the museum or furnish copies as needed for research or exhibition purposes.

Fuertes found Africa an ornithologist's paradise and an artist's dream, for the birds were colorful, plentiful and, for him, entirely new. In a letter written home from a 10,000-foot elevation on Mt. Albasso, he described the diversity of species found in just one of the many areas the group explored:

> Here the characteristic things are ravens—great croaking buzzards with a white nape and deep heavy bill that light on the backs of sore mules and eat the raw live flesh of the poor things; eagles of several kinds, vultures, and the great 'Lammergeyer,' a bearded vulture, one of the largest birds in the world, and a most monstrous-fine flier; kites, a large white-breasted hawk; Bateleur eagles; on the barer parts of the hills francolins like huge quail, of two kinds, give most beautiful shooting and delicious food; doves of several kinds hoot, grunt, coo, or rattle in the boscage, according to their individual wont (or will).[59]

During the eight-month trip, Fuertes painted the most interesting of these and other birds encountered, focusing, as he always did, on those with conspicuous fleshy parts, the colors of which would be lost in death. As the months went on, vultures, kites, shrikes, kingfishers, and dozens of other birds came to life in the pages of his 11-x-15-inch sketch pads. His fellow travelers and the many strangers who saw his work—including Haile Selassie, the Abyssinian Emperor—gasped at the beauty of the paintings and marveled at their accuracy. Fuertes, too, was pleased with the studies, as he revealed in a letter to George Sutton on his return:

> We had a marvelous trip in Abyssinia, and among other things I got far the best lot of field studies I ever did on one trip; a hundred color studies and a lot of drawings. Many of the birds most curious and bizarre.[60]

In late August of 1927, just a few months after his homecoming, Fuertes and his wife drove to Tannersville, New York to show the Abyssinian paintings to Frank Chapman and his wife. It was the last time Fuertes would discuss his work with anyone, for on the return trip his car was struck by a train, and the artist was instantly killed. Mrs. Fuertes was severely burned; the bundle of pictures was flung away from the car and escaped injury.[61]

The Abyssinian paintings were purchased in their entirety and presented to the Chicago Field Museum by C. Suydam Cutting, a wealthy patron who had participated in the Abyssinian expedition as a volunteer. Three years later, also with Mr. Cutting's support, a portfolio of thirty-two birds and mammals from the collection was reproduced by the Field Museum as a slipcased set of individual prints. While the Abyssinian studies are unquestionably among Fuertes' best works, one reason they are more famous than his earlier paintings is that they are among the very few Fuertes study sketches that are widely reproduced. Until publication of these paintings, none of Fuertes' "unfinished" works had been seen. The public had formed its opinion of Fuertes from illustrations that were often badly reproduced in books and magazines. In 1930, when the Abyssinian portfolio appeared, the freshness and spontaneity of the studies came as a revelation, and Fuertes' reputation took another well-deserved leap forward. Subsequent publication of Fuertes' study sketches in Mary Boynton's *Louis Agassiz Fuertes* (1956) and Frederick George Marcham's *Louis Agassiz Fuertes and the Singular Beauty*

Barn Owl
Tyto alba
Watercolor, 15″ × 11″

of Birds (1971) has revealed Fuertes' real mastery at capturing the essence of a bird in life.

Although Louis Agassiz Fuertes was more comfortable observing birds and painting pictures than theorizing about art, he followed a consistent artistic credo throughout his career. It was articulated in a letter to young artist Conrad Roland in 1925, stressing truth and objectivity over personal statement:

> I'm sure I don't know what to say to you about your work and your attitude toward it, and the ideals that prompt you, except for God's sake be honest, and strive for what seems to you true and lovely. I should say that more high aspiration has been egoized into mediocrity than has withstood the terrible ordeal of passing through a human soul for its interpretation. Art, as a means of expression of the ego, is like playing a symphony on a Jew's harp, in nine hundred and ninety-nine cases out of a thousand (count 'em), and I think a man in our field . . . can well go on to sixty plus with pure study and representation before beginning to get fancy. I am aware that ninety-nine percent of the artists and all the critics, who earn their living by their vocabulary, are agin me in this, and would scorn such art as I like as photographic (as if it were a scrofulous imitation) but I still stick out for knowledge—good, sound, deep, and appreciative knowledge—as the one fundamental basic prerequisite of all art, and particularly of naturalistic art. There haven't been ten people in all history that have had it, and the outlook isn't too bright for the future, but that is no detriment to the pursuit of it, and the fellow that lands will eventually have the world at his feet, which will probably bore him to death. Great lovers have all had their admiring audience; great lovers of natural truth perhaps less than others. But that is my simple credo: it's easy, however, to 'believe' in truth, as an abstract conception; quite another thing to discover and crystallize this truth into visible and permanent form. That's a hard job, and most artists would rather pass the buck, and in place of hard-wrought unadorned truth, present the gog-eyed world with the decorative by-products of their efforts, not so much for truth as for originality. As the vehicle for truth, originality is fine; as the mere expression of half-baked ego it is a flop, as witness any fall exhibition after the silly season.[62]

Fuertes attributed many of his truth-seeking habits and his abilities to express them to his teacher Abbott Thayer. He remained forever indebted to Thayer for what he called an "emancipation" from perceiving the subtleties of the natural world by habit to "real seeing."[63] "The only way I can think of to even up the balance at all," he wrote, "is to pass on when I can, to other boys who come into my reach with any kind of eye-hunger for these things that get so deeply to you and yours and me, something of the help that you so wonderfully and freely gave me. . . ."[64] Pass them along he did.

THE FUERTES INFLUENCE

Throughout his thirty years of professional painting, Fuertes was the model of generosity, always willing to take time from his pressing schedule to help a child—or adult—with painting, field identification, or any number of other projects. Some younger artists he helped more by inspiration than

Eastern Phoebe
Sayornis phoebe
Watercolor
8″ × 6″

instruction, or through brief personal encounters. Such was the case with Roger Tory Peterson, who would revolutionize bird-watching techniques with the publication of his *Field Guide to the Birds* in 1934. Peterson met Fuertes at an AOU congress in 1925 and never forgot the experience. Terrance Shortt, now considered the dean of Canadian bird painters, recalls saving his pennies as a teenager so he could attend his first AOU meeting for the purpose of meeting Fuertes. He was devastated by the news of Fuertes' death just a few months before the trip, and canceled his reservations.[65] Other artists, like Keith Shaw Williams, Courtenay Brandreth, and Conrad Roland, benefited from personal instruction and years of correspondence.

The artist who most directly benefited from Fuertes' generosity, however, was George Miksch Sutton, today regarded as one of America's best bird painters. In early 1915, after years of distant admiration, a seventeen-year-old Sutton wrote Fuertes to express his appreciation of the elder artist's work and to tell him of his own interests in bird painting. Thus began a close personal and professional relationship that would last for the rest of Fuertes'

95

life. The correspondence between the two men, recently published in Sutton's *To a Young Bird Artist; Letters from Louis Agassiz Fuertes to George Miksch Sutton* (1979), reveals much about Fuertes' artistic methods and beliefs, and offers useful instructions to aspiring bird artists.

Following young Sutton's first letter, Fuertes invited him to visit the family at their summer home at Sheldrake on Lake Cayuga. Typically, he refused any suggestion of payment for his instruction:

> . . . In case everything goes as you hope and you come and I'm here, the matter of "lessons" need not worry you at all. I have no secret processes or other patents on this profession, and I should consider it a privilege to pass on to you what little of the help and encouragement I could of all that has been so freely lavished on me by my good friends in days and years now past, and if I should myself seek reward for so poorly doing what was so richly done for me, I should in truth feel like a worse parasite than I hope I shall ever have to feel! If you should come, you will be allowed to pay for everything you get, except such help and criticism as I can give you while you are here: *that*, at least, you cannot pay for, because it will be no trouble at all, and I shall be, as I have said, only too happy to help you along.[66]

Traveling by train from West Virginia to Sheldrake Point, Sutton lived with the Fuertes family just as Fuertes had done with the Thayers so many years before. Fortunately for Sutton, he came during one of the few summers when Fuertes was painting at Sheldrake. "Day after day I watched and learned from Fuertes," recalls Sutton. "I was not with him all the time, but usually I was within calling distance. . . ."[67]

Despite pressing deadlines on the two commissions then under way ("The Larger North American Mammals" for the *National Geographic* and nine drawings of common birds for John Dryden Kuser's *The Way to Study Birds* (1917)), Fuertes took time to instruct Sutton on new painting techniques and the principles of accurately seeing light and color. During a brief visit to his Ithaca studio, he showed Sutton reproductions of the work of British bird painter Archibald Thorburn and Swedish artist Bruno Liljefors, praising their respective mastery of feather texture and habitat depiction. (Interestingly, these were the very same artists whose originals he discussed with Roger Tory Peterson at the time of their meeting a decade later.)[68]

Sutton eagerly absorbed the instruction he received during the summer of 1916 and subsequently. He spent much of his life incorporating the artistic principles learned from Fuertes into his own outstanding work. "Suppose someone were asked to pick from my work ten drawings showing the influence of Fuertes on me," wrote Sutton in 1949. "Said person could choose as he pleased, for practically every drawing I have done as a mature person has shown in one way or another the Fuertes influence."[69]

Roger Tory Peterson has suggested that Fuertes' influence can be seen in the work of most of North America's leading bird painters to this day. While many of the "Fuertes School" of painters have gone on to develop distinctive styles of their own, few would not acknowledge their debt to the master of ornithological portraiture.

Peregrine Falcon, *Falco peregrinus,* with Green-winged Teal, *Anas carolinensis,* Watercolor, 13″ × 9″

Maroon-tailed Parakeet
Pyrrhura melanura,
and White-necked Parakeet
Pyrrhura albipectus
Watercolor
11″ × 15″

Part III

The Naturalist

Louis Fuertes once joked that his love of travel was so intense that even the sight of a map "starts me sweating inside, and renders me generally unfit for the purpose of a provider."[1] In fact, it was his extensive field experience that made his work so valuable.

Fuertes believed that birds had to be carefully observed in the wild to be fully understood and properly painted. He also recognized the transient nature of certain pigments that characterized living species:

> Almost all water birds, the birds of prey, and many land birds have colors in life, and especially at the breeding season, which cannot in any known way be preserved. The bills of many ducks are varied and bright in color and often swollen or queer in form which shrink and dry dull colored in a specimen. The skin about the eyes and the eyes themselves of the hawks are often bright and unexpected colors. All such characteristics must be painted carefully from either living or freshly shot birds. . . .[2]

Fuertes considered his field notes and paintings "the most important and valuable part" of his equipment,[3] and maintained them, along with his own collection of study skins, as a permanent reference library for his finished work.

Fortunately, Fuertes was never without opportunities to expand his knowledge of bird life through the firsthand observation he advocated. Beginning with his trip to Florida with Abbott Thayer, Gerald Thayer, and Charles Knight in 1898, Fuertes enjoyed a virtually unbroken string of valuable field experiences. The most important of these are described below.

ALASKA—1899

The Harriman Alaska Expedition of 1899, organized and financed by Edward Henry Harriman under circumstances described in Part I, was clearly the most luxurious of Fuertes' trips. It was also the largest expedition in which Fuertes would ever participate. Besides a crew of sixty-five officers and men and an additional force of eleven hunters, packers, and campers to assist the landing parties, the Harrimans took physicians, stenographers, a chaplain, a nurse, and four family servants. The scientific staff of thirty was comprised of many of the country's leading botanists, zoologists, geologists,

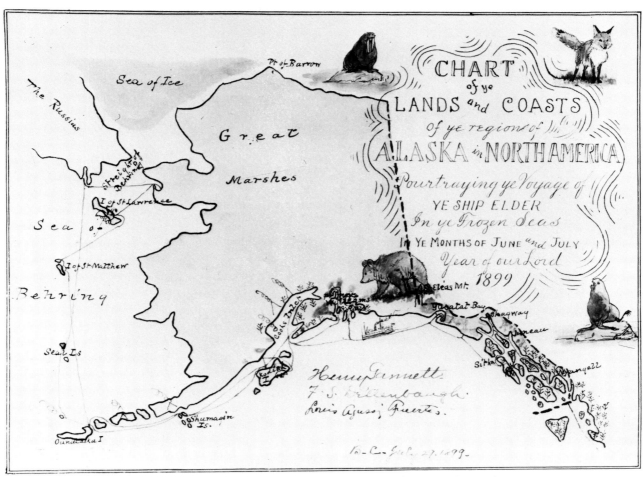

The route of the Harriman Alaska Expedition as drawn by Henry Gannett (Chief geographer, United States Geological Survey), Frederick S. Dellenbaugh (artist), and Louis Agassiz Fuertes, for Mrs. Harriman's scrapbook, 1899.

artists, photographers, "and at least one dreamer," as John Burroughs modestly described himself. The rest of the party was made up of Harriman guests and relatives, including seven-year-old Averell Harriman, the youngest on the expedition. The trip's provisions, no less complete than the staff, ran the gamut from launches, canoes, and camping equipment to fresh fruit and livestock. Burroughs explained:

> We have hunting parties among us that expect to supply us with venison and bear meat, but to be on the safe side we take aboard eleven fat steers, a flock of sheep, chickens and turkeys, a milch cow [for the Harriman children], and a span of horses. . . . The hold of our ship looked like a farmer's barnyard."[4]

Assigned a comfortable cabin below decks, Fuertes quickly arranged for additional work space. With the help of the Harriman daughters, he secured a studio "right up in the skylights over the engine room—a place painted white, with a course of windows all around and skylights overhead."[5] It was, all agreed, the finest studio on the ship.

100

The S.S. *George W. Elder* and its distinguished passengers left Seattle on May 31, 1899, amid much celebration by the local citizens. The ship steamed north past Vancouver Island, Lowe Inlet, and Wrangell, through scenery that Fuertes described as "much more magnificent than anything I have ever seen." While the others settled into shipboard life and awaited the expedition's major stops, Fuertes and the two senior ornithologists aboard—A. K. Fisher of the Biological Survey and Robert Ridgway, ornithologist for the Smithsonian and president of the American Ornithologists' Union—began their inventory of birds from deck and on their occasional short trips to shore. The first specimen collected was a common raven, a species Fuertes found "astonishingly common" and tame. "They are great devilish jokers," he wrote, "who give you a jolly and then chuckle, peep, whistle, grunt, croak, bark, cackle, gobble and everything else about it."[6] He found rufous hummingbirds equally abundant, and enjoyed watching them when ashore:

> [It is] the strangest thing to see a bright fox-colored hummingbird s-s-sing like a creeper, with a big bumble-bee buzz—curve up into a giant forest, where everything in view is vast; poise with its tail, pendulum-like, swinging under it, look around and 'brooooooom' off again, all before you notice it! Or to hear a little undertone hum, look up, and see through the leaves of a red-flowered blackberry bush a tiny white-throated female looking at you solicitously for a scared second, and quietly fade away.[7]

John Burroughs (left) and John Muir explore the flora, fauna, and geology of Alaska during a stop of the S.S. *George W. Elder*.

Fuertes' sketches of the birds seen and collected, posted in the ship's "Social Hall" by Mrs. Harriman, were widely admired by the other passengers. "They look quite pretty," remarked Fuertes in a letter home, "but are of course only rough studies, and not very much like the birds they bluff at."[8]

After brief stops at Wrangell and Skagway, the party made an extended visit to Glacier Bay, where the scientists enjoyed five days of observation and collection. It was a particularly dramatic site, and provided the first opportunity for land-based surveys by the scientists aboard. Fuertes, who was especially taken by the grandeur of the glaciers, described the *Elder*'s arrival in the bay with an account that draws on every sense but smell:

> At two in the P.M. it grew noticeably and quickly colder, and by three, when we came in good view of the splendid Muir Glacier, it was really wintry. This is a vast Niagara of ice—coming down to the sea between two great mountains—and divided by an 'island' mountain. . . . The color of the deep ice is beyond belief, not green-blue as I had expected it, but a high value bright clear *blue*, like bluing. The face is between 180 and 220 ft. high and probably a mile long and the whole like a great river. It moves ten feet a day in the middle and every few minutes or seconds a great piece will scale away with a report of a great cannon, strike the water with a roar, send spray sometimes as high as the face of the ice cliff, force up an immense foaming wave which floods across the bay, breaking up in roaring surf half a mile from where it started.[9]

The S.S. *George W. Elder* (r) and a three-masted whaling schooner in Orea Harbor at 11:00 P.M. Photograph by Edward S. Curtis.

Common Raven
Corvus corax
Pencil study
8″ × 10″

Debarking from the ship, Fuertes and his colleagues set up camp on the Gustavus Peninsula, "a long, low, wooded stretch of land twenty miles below Muir Glacier."[10] Fuertes described the stop:

Dr. Fernow, Dr. Fisher, Robert Ridgway, Kearny, and I and Cole are in camp at last. We got in about noon, made camp, got lunch and went out. It is a most ideal spot, the woods are most beautiful, deep in soft moss, so that one makes no sound in going through them, and the trunks are covered with light blue-gray mosses and lichens, so that the colors are soft and harmonious. . . . The blowing and snorting of the whales, the screaming, way out on the bay of gulls and loons, and an occasional goose, and near by, the licking of the little waves in the pebbles and hum of a big bee, with just a thin 'ray' of the hermit's song way over across the bay in the spruces, make the part of the picture that you see with your ears. The other part goes beyond my vocabulary, which has gradually become dwindled down to Wow and Gee. . . . We shall probably be here a day or two more—I'd like to make it a week or ten days, as I'm soft from much food and sleep and little exercise on board the good ship Geo. W. Elder, which feeds us too well.[11]

The expedition's five-day visit to Glacier Bay and Muir Glacier was among the most important of its stops. Henry Gannett's careful mappings of the glaciers, Edward Curtis' photographs, and the data gathered by John

103

Muir and the rest of the party would become an invaluable historical record; a few weeks after the expedition's close, a major earthquake in the region altered its appearance forever.

Weighing anchor on June 13th, after what Muir described as "a perfectly glorious time in Glacier Bay—five days of the most splendid weather I ever saw in Alaska,"[12] the party sailed south to Sitka, and old trading town surrounded by steep, spruce-covered mountains.

After the Sitka visit and several days in Yakutat Bay, the *Elder* moved north again to Prince William Sound. There the expedition examined and named glaciers in honor of Columbia, Harvard, Yale, Radcliffe, Smith, Bryn Mawr, Vassar, Wellesley, and Amherst. Highlighting their Sound survey was the discovery of a fjord, about twelve miles long, through which Harriman boldly guided the *Elder* despite the objections of the ship's pilot and captain. While Burroughs, Muir, and most of the geologists aboard considered this the trip's most exciting experience, and Harriman (for whom the fjord was quickly named) looked back on it with tremendous pride, Fuertes found the episode less thrilling than his daily exposure to new birds. A letter describing his brief visit to Unalaska on July 10th is typical:

> At Unalaska, a most interesting place, we lay to to water and coal, and Fisher and I piled right ashore to hunt, and were filled with new sensations right away. Some of the loveliest birds, whose names had become familiar, but which had in themselves become myths, were found to be very common, and easily obtainable, and their singing brought one back to the bobolink-filled meadows of the east. The Lapland longspurs were the finest singers, and among the most beautiful. The beautiful rosy finches, or leucostictes, were also quite common, but shy after the first shot, so that I didn't get many, though I'd like to have gotten them for the Thayers. I got an owl, new to me, the short-ear, and the type song-sparrow.[13]

Eskimos in Umiak circle the S.S. *George W. Elder*, Port Clarence, Alaska, during the Harriman Alaska Expedition, 1899.

After a long trip through the Bering Sea with stops at the Pribilof Islands, Plover Bay (Siberia), and Port Clarence, the *Elder* started its return voyage. "I begin to feel as if my face were turned homeward," wrote Fuertes from Popoff Island on July 18th, "and it's not a bad feeling, though I've had good luck and a bully time. I've got ninety-five skins put up, and a portfolio full of studies, and I suppose that a dozen more of each will about conclude this trip's work."[14]

Despite the many exciting experiences he had had on the outward trip, it was a stop at Hall Island on the return that Fuertes considered "by far and away the most interesting place we have seen."[15] He described his visit to the island in a letter home:

> . . . We got there at about 7, and having had dinner early, a lot of us went ashore at once. We had seen many sea birds around the island and found that the cliffs were densely populated with nine or ten species of sea birds: one of those wonderful sights that I had heard and read so much about. But all descriptions failed utterly to make the impression that the thing warranted, as it is truly the most wonderful sight I've ever seen. Thousands and thousands of birds—tame to stupidity, seated on every little ledge or projection—from the size of sandpipers up to a great white gull that spreads five feet—all the time coming and going, screaming, croaking, peeping, chuckling, with constant moving of countless heads—all where you can reach over the cliff and catch the birds from the top in your hands—makes a wonderful sight, and one not soon to be forgotten. . . .[16]

Long-tailed Jaegers in flight
Stercorarius longicaudus
Black-and-white lithograph
5″ × 7½″
From an original wash
now lost

105

Harlequin Quail
Cyrtonyx montezumae
Wash, 11¾″ × 7¼″
Texas, 1901

When the *Elder* arrived in Seattle on July 30th, she had traveled 9,000 miles. "We had three tons of coal left in our bunkers," reported Burroughs, "but of our little stock farm down below only the milch cow remained. . . . No voyagers were ever more fortunate than we. No storms, no winds, no delays nor accidents to speak of, no illness. We had gone far and fared well."[17]

The expedition left its mark on science in the form of hundreds of newly discovered insect, plant, and mammal species, scores of scientific papers, and a fifteen-volume report published jointly in 1901 by the Washington Academy of Sciences and the Smithsonian Institution. Its mark on the participants was less tangible but no less profound. The 126 members of the expedition, strangers two months before, were now a close-knit group of friends. As the members went their separate ways, each reflected on the remarkable experiences they had shared. John Muir summarized the feelings of most participants in a letter to the Harrimans' daughters:

Dear Girls:
I received your kind compound letter from the railroad washout with great pleasure, for it showed, as I fondly thought, that no wreck, washout or crevasse of any sort will be likely to break or wash out the memories of our group trip, or abate the friendliness that sprung up on the Elder among the wild scenery of Alaska during these last two memorable months. No doubt every one of the favored happy band feels, as I do, that this was the grandest trip of his life. To me it was particularly grateful and interesting because nearly all of my life I have wandered and studied alone. On the Elder, I found not only the fields I liked best to study, but a hotel, a club, and a home, together with a floating university in which I enjoyed the instruction and companionship of a lot of the best fellows imaginable, culled and arranged like a well-balanced bouquet, or like a band of glaciers flowing smoothly together, each in its own channel, or perhaps at times like a lot of round boulders merrily swirling and chafing against each other in a glacier pothole. . . .[18]

Muir regretted that "so rare a company should have to be broken, never to be assembled again," but other members of the group, sharing his fear, were determined to keep their Alaskan friendships intact. "The H.A.E. (termed in full—Ham and Eggs) has resolved itself into the Ham and Eggs Club with Mr. H. president," wrote Fuertes from Seattle. The club, he continued, was "to meet in full as possible once a year in New York and as often as it wants in 2's and 3's and anywhere."[19]

Fuertes, one of the most active members of the club, continued to keep up his friendships with expedition members long after the trip's close. A. K. Fisher became a frequent correspondent; less than five months after the *Elder*'s return, Fuertes was suggesting that the two team up for another trip. "Just le me know your plans," he wrote, ". . . and perhaps we can do up the Rio Grande, or the Bahamas, or Yucatan, or the Philippines, or some place."[20] The suggestions were surprisingly prophetic, for by the close of the decade Fuertes had made expeditions to three of the four sites mentioned. Although Fisher did not participate in any of the three, through his influence with the United States Biological Survey he was probably partly responsible for Fuertes' inclusion in the first of three trips: the government's Texas study of 1901.

TEXAS—1901

Fuertes arrived in San Antonio on April 13, 1901, with a trunk of clothes, shells, and other supplies; a chest of camping equipment; and a letter of introduction to two army officers stationed at nearby Fort Sam Houston. With their help, he secured a room in a small house on the edge of town, where he was pleased to discover he could "shoot without making a row."[21] His instructions from Vernon Bailey of the Biological Survey were to make whatever ornithological collections he could, then travel west to rendezvous with Harry Oberholser and Bailey at a location and time still to be determined. In short, he was on his own to see and do what he liked, at the government's expense.

Fuertes wasted no time in these endeavors, as can be seen from the series of roadrunner studies completed on the day of his arrival. He found the birds in San Antonio "thick and interesting,"[22] with the scissor-tailed flycatcher at the top of his list:

> The scissor-tail flycatchers are the most striking and about the most beautiful birds around. They are very common like robins at home and about the size of kingbirds with 10 inch tails with 6 inches of fork in them. They have all the kingbird habits of darting up, fighting in air, diving, dashing off after a bug, etc., and are so light gray that they are almost white, with dark wings and tail and the sides of the body under the wings orange vermillion!! which washes out into peachy pink on the flanks and suffuses the gray of the back. They look like Roman candles in the daytime when they fly by with the afternoon sun getting under and lighting them. Sometimes ten or more will all dash up into the air and squabble together, opening and shutting their great rocket tipped tails. . . .[23]

At the end of five days, he had collected samples of all of the local birds— "25 or 30 skins—some of them prizes, all of them nice,"[24]—and was ready to move on to new terrain. Traveling west by train, he spent two days in Uvalde, where he "found some splendid things . . . and kept the house more or less in meat with blue-winged teal and scaled partridge. Also got a lovely oriole and a pair of fine little queer woodpeckers among many other things."[25]

Going further west to Comstock, then north to Langtry, Fuertes added to his growing collection, and reveled in the novelty of the land and its bird life. "As for my own state of being," he reassured his parents,

> I have been as well as it is possible to be every minute and the little bottles of medicine are still unmolested. Except for the fair denizens of the mattress in San Antonio [a plague of biting insects], I haven't lost a minute's sleep since I left home, and my health is, as per usual, perfect. . . . My beard is beginning to get back into form—two weeks now—and I look like a real nice miner. But don't worry; it will either be good or off when I come home.[26]

108

Black Phoebe, *Sayornis nigricans,* Wash, 8½″ × 6¾″

Canyon Wren
Catherpes mexicanus
Wash
8¾″ × 5½″
Texas, 1901

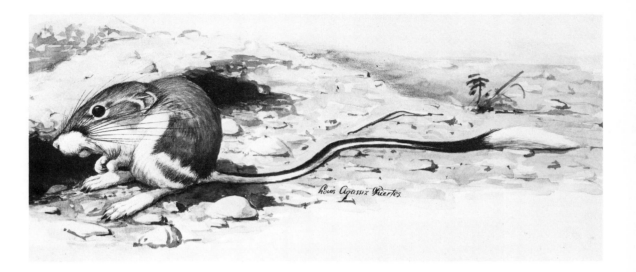

Bannertail Kangaroo Rat
Dipodomys spectabilis
Wash
11" × 14"

While he found much of western Texas "as barren as an ashpile, except for cactus, aloe and such things as Mezquite and chaparal,"[27] Fuertes marveled at the beauty of its canyons:

> The cañons are the places to go. . . . While there are lots of birds and other interesting things to be seen and heard up on the plains, the cañons form, from their improved water conditions, the finest kind of refuge for all the things that would like the climate of the country if it weren't so dry. These "bottoms" are generally grassy, between the rocks, and have good sized trees, live oaks and some others, which the birds like, and the rocks give fine places for hawks, eagles, cañon and rock wrens and other things to nest in.
>
> A cardinal or cañon wren can certainly make the whole big cañon ring with its song and it seems wonderful to hear a great clanging whistle, like a boy through his fingers, running from high up, right down the scale, in clear deliberate notes—and look up and see near the top of a 200 foot cliff—perhaps 50 or more yards up the cañon, a bird the size of a chippy [chipping sparrow] climbing around like a nuthatch on the rock face—the author of the thing. You can hear their song a good quarter of a mile if not more.[28]

Rising at dawn each day, the young artist explored the canyons and countryside during the cool, early morning hours, then returned to the house or tent in which he was living to skin the birds he had collected, write up his field notes, and paint the birds he'd seen. This quick conversion not only enabled him to record the proper lifelike colors of each species, but also assured a greater accuracy of pose and setting in his work than if he had waited to paint the birds in his studio.

After almost two weeks on his own, Fuertes was glad to meet up with Oberholser and Bailey to begin the survey of the fauna of the Rio Grande and the Chisos Mountains, which he considered "the real object of the trip." "These days are crammed with wonder and work,"[29] he noted in early May.

Gila Woodpecker
Centurus uropygialis
Wash
11″ × 14″

"Time goes flying and is just as full of interest as the air is full of new sounds and smells, and the queer little animals that O and B bring in tempt me to draw them very often."[30]

By the second week of June, Fuertes had collected more than two-hundred specimens and had discovered six bird species previously unrecorded in Texas.[31] He had also seen a great number of other creatures native to the Chisos Mountains, the most startling of which he described in a letter to his family:

> The other day I was coming out of the gulch after an unsuccessful day, when I saw what seemed at first to be a dry oak leaf, walking down a little leafy place between some loose stones, and it proved, on being l-l-l-l-looked at under the k-k-k-kitchen l-l-l-lamp to be the biggest tarantula that any of us ever saw. I don't honestly think he would go on my extended hand all stretched out—I chucked him in formelin and will send him on as a token of my slight esteem some day.[32]

Despite this experience and encounters with scorpions earlier in the trip, Fuertes relished the rigors of camp life. "The grub and the work make a product that seems to fit my constitution perfectly," he proclaimed.[33]

> Bailey laughs at me for refusing to get under a tree at night instead of lugging my bunk[?] out into the open mountain meadow—but I wouldn't miss the cool breeze on my head and the wonderful throbbing bigness of these glorious nights for anything he could name.[34]

Greater Antillean Grackle
Quiscalus niger
Wash
9½″ × 12½″

Pygmy Nuthatch
Sitta pygmaea
Watercolor
8″ × 5″
Texas, 1901

After a month of successful collecting in the Chisos Mountains, the Bailey outfit (complete with cook, packhorses, and supplies) moved on to the Davis Mountains and then divided up, with Fuertes making a solo trip into the Sacramento Mountains of New Mexico:

> . . . at about 9 [I] got aboard the little short-car train that climbs up the 5,000 ft. between El Paso and Cloudcroft. It took 'till 7 that night to get there, but a more wonderful ride I never took. It is 128 miles and the first 100 is over very gradually rising plains—past the Organ Mountains, then the San Andreas range, both 15 or 20 miles to the westward of us. . . . Well, [from Alamogordo] it took from 1:45 to 7 to go the 28 miles to Cloudcroft and the first 10 is over level land and we made good time on it. But the last 18 is the most wonderful series of curves, loops, Y switches and twists, and all on a grade running from 3 to 10 feet in a hundred, and takes you up through a big gulch, from side to side, up into cañons and out a higher level, climbing steadily up and up; through zone after zone of vegetation—scrubby Mezquite first, then into a few oaks, junipers, pines, which increase in size as you go higher, past fertile stream-spread valley lands, rank with weeds and grasses, until finally you come to immense pine and spruce trees, virgin in their denseness and beauty.[35]

Fuertes was enchanted by the Sacramentos. He stayed there for six days, hunting in the magnificent spruce forests each morning and working in his

114

Streak-backed Oriole, *Icterus pustulatus*, Watercolor, 11″ × 8″

Short-eared Owl
Asio flammeus
Watercolor, 14″ × 11″

tent each afternoon. By contrast to "the delicious moist coolness of the Sacramento forests," El Paso was a "seething Hell" that he was delighted to leave on August 3rd.[36]

In Carlsbad, New Mexico, he rejoined Vernon Bailey, who was now accompanied by his wife, Florence Merriam Bailey, the sister of C. Hart Merriam and the author of *A-Birding on a Bronco*, the first published book that Fuertes had illustrated. The purpose of his visit was to discuss details for illustrating Mrs. Bailey's next book, *Handbook of Birds of the Western United States*, which was to become the companion volume to Frank Chapman's classic *Handbook of Birds of Eastern North America*. After a successful meeting, some additional fieldwork with Vernon Bailey, and a visit with an old college friend whose family owned the Vineyard Ranch in Carlsbad, Fuertes traveled east to Washington, New York City, and home.

THE BAHAMAS—1902

"There are larger birds than the Flamingo, and birds with more brilliant plumage, but no other large bird is so brightly colored and no other brightly colored bird is so large."[37] So wrote Frank Chapman in *Camps and Cruises of an Ornightologist* in describing the primary objective of the American Museum of Natural History's expedition to the Bahamas. While the flamingo had long been recognized as a remarkably beautiful bird, little or nothing was known of its nesting habits in the wild. Chapman's goal was to "lift the veil through which the Flamingo's home life has been but dimly seen"[38] by examining its nesting colonies firsthand.

The expedition, consisting of Dr. and Mrs. Frank Chapman, Mr. and Mrs. J. Lewis Bonhote, Louis Fuertes, and a native crew of seven, left Nassau aboard the sixty-foot schooner *Estrella* on April 22, 1902. Just three days into the trip, however, Chapman contracted measles and had to return to Nassau, aborting the party's plans to visit Inagua.

While Chapman recuperated in an abandoned lunatic ward of the Colonial Hospital, flanked by a leper compound and quarters for the insane, Fuertes and Bonhote, a British ornithologist and one-time secretary to the governor of the Bahamas, explored southern Andros island and the adjacent keys for the rich variety of seabirds found there.

Pencil study, Short-eared Owl (right) with Peregrine Falcon *(Falco peregrinus)*, 8″ × 10″ (see p. 97)

Fuertes reported to Abbott Thayer that the two men "did well with what time was left to us—and saw noddies, sooties, royal, cabots, bridled, gull–billed and least terns, most of them in great numbers."[39] They also visited and photographed a flamingo nesting colony with over fifteen hundred nests, but as they were too early for the breeding season, they were unable to see the "Flamingo City" in use.

Fuertes took full opportunity of his flamingo observations then and in the years to come. He drew hundreds of the birds in a large background mural for a Bird Hall habitat group in the American Museum of Natural History, and later, after a subsequent visit to the Bahamas in 1920, created menu, stationery designs, and a mural for the luxurious Flamingo Hotel in Miami Beach, Florida.

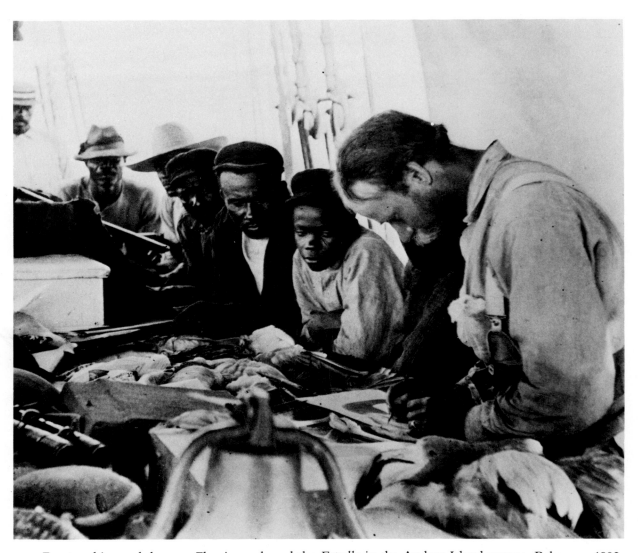

Fuertes skins and draws a Flamingo aboard the *Estrella* in the Andros Island waters, Bahamas, 1902.

While working on the hotel project, he painted several large oils of flamingos, including one commissioned by the New York Zoological Society. The painting was enthusiastically received by the zoo's director, William Hornaday, in May 1921:

American Flamingo
Phoenicopterus ruber
Oil
27¾″ × 50″
1924

Dear Mr. Fuertes:

Your great flamingo painting arrived yesterday spick and span, debonaire and perfectly preserved. It hangs in the place of honor in our main reception room and I regard it as tremendously successful. I think that it marks the beginning of a new departure in pictures of American birds and I am glad that I have lived to see the day. With this before me what is the use of going to Andros Island to see flamingoes?

The wonderful fidelity with which you have reproduced the spirit of the tropics and the motif of the flamingo at home is beyond all ordinary terms of praise. The birds are magnificent, or at least Dr. Beebe says so, and he is a severe critic of things that are criticizable. Your mangroves are absolutely the real thing. The cabbage palmettos are very much to my mind. The flying flock completes the tale of birds.[40]

Frank Chapman was so pleased with Fuertes' work on the Bird Hall flamingo diorama that he included him in a number of other trips to gather specimens and background ideas for bird displays in the museum.

119

Los Banos, Cal
June 17-03
Young Cinnamon Teal

Teal

L.A.F.

Young Cinnamon Teal
Anas cyanoptera
Watercolor
6″ × 6¾″
California, 1903

In 1907 the two men collected birds in the prairies of Saskatchewan and the mountains of Alberta, and in 1908 they explored the Cuthbert Rookery in southern Florida with ornithologist Arthur Cleveland Bent.

Other trips made by Fuertes during this period included an AOU excursion to Nevada, New Mexico, Colorado, and California in the early summer of 1903; his wedding trip to Jamaica (arranged with the help of Frank Chapman) in 1904; and a month-long collecting trip to the Magdalen Islands in the Gulf of Saint Lawrence in 1909. The Magdalen Island expedition was organized and financed by Dr. and Mrs. Leonard C. Sanford of New Haven, Connecticut, enthusiastic amateurs who were generous in their support of ornithological study at the Museum of Natural History and elsewhere. The number and variety of seabirds the group saw during its visit to the Magdalens—and particularly on the Bird Rocks—were literally overwhelming, as Fuertes reported in a letter to his wife:

> I can't describe the rocks to you, but the excitement of seeing thousands of great gannets nesting on the ledges, and hearing their croaking and the screaming of the myriad Kittiwake gulls was exhausting, and I found it very bewildering to know where to commence. But we did commence, and I soon had my day's work staked out. I painted all morning and skinned all afternoon and evening.[41]

120

Field glass sketches. (Chicks hidden near)

Black-necked Stilts

Los Banos, Cal
May 23, 1903

Black-necked Stilt, *Himantopus mexicanus,* 11¾″ × 9½″, California, 1903

Atlantic Puffin, *Fratercula arctica*, Watercolor study, 12″ × 9¼″, Magdalen Islands, 1909

Burrowing Owl
Speotyto cunicularia
Watercolor
13½″ × 10″

YUCATAN, MEXICO—1910

Less than three months after his return from the Gulf of Saint Lawrence, Fuertes received an invitation to join Chapman on a museum expedition to the Yucatan Peninsula. The focus of the trip was Mt. Orizaba (Citlaltepetl), an 18,000-foot volcano with habitat zones ranging from tropical to arctic and supporting an accordingly varied bird population.

Establishing a base in Cordoba, a small town at the foot of the mountain, in early March, the ornithologists spent almost a month studying birds and

123

gathering specimens in the immediate vicinity. In a letter of March 21st, Fuertes described their activities:

> We have been making the best of the bad weather by side trips to various points along the down-end of the line. Motzorongo twice, where a regular hothouse condition of life exists: perfectly gigantic forests of silk-cotton and wild fig, with curious small palms and tremendous ferns, climbing vines like a ship's rigging everywhere, from wire size to the thickness of your body—reeking, steaming, moist, and where live trogons, toucans, parrots, all sorts of tanagers and hummers, queer new and unimagined birds, jaguars and even monkeys, and orchids of all sorts and colors, air plants un-nameable, odorous of queer flowers and reeking with strange and very impressive smells, silent except for unguessable bird-notes. If it weren't for an old trail that follows the stream, it would be impenetrable: as it is it is a perfectly ideal collecting ground (except for the sweltering dampness and the mosquitoes) and more than anything else like a limitless hothouse of wildly strange exotic plants.[42]

Eager to explore the higher reaches of Orizaba, Chapman and Fuertes, along with an assistant named Patterson, left their hotel in Cordoba and traveled—first by train, then by horse—to a campsite 7,000 feet up the mountain, where the party was the object of "keen interest, not to say open amusement" to the Indians living nearby.[43] The following morning they

Fuertes examines a well-camouflaged ptarmigan, Alberta, Canada, 1907. Photograph by Frank Chapman.

Emerald Toucanet
Aulacorhynchus prasinus
Watercolor
9″ × 12¾″

pushed on through the "corn belt" and into the "zone of pines." The trail, Fuertes explained, ran "the entire distance along the top of a knife-like ridge, or hog-back, twenty-one miles long, with deep barrancas on each side; so that as we were in the clouds all the time, and could frequently look from our horses down into eternity on both sides, the sensation was much as I should suppose ballooning would be."[44] After a second night's camp at 9,500 feet, the party pushed on to a final campsite at 12,000 feet, which, as Fuertes observed, "was too high, for at night, when the sun set, the thermometer dropped in fifteen minutes from 57 degrees to 12 degrees and we suffered . . . from cold. Before noon next day, the mercury in the sun was 112 degrees. 100 degrees' change in twelve hours!"[45]

Despite the occasional hardships of the climate, their Mt. Orizaba survey—and ascent—was extremely successful, resulting in many fine specimens and drawings. Fuertes found thė temporary transition back into city life more difficult than dealing with the rigors of the wild, as he revealed in a postcard to his wife:

Mexico City isn't much to one so ignorant of Mexico City as I am, and I find myself very keen to get down to the lagoon at Tampico, and on the trail. We've had such wonderful times in great untouched forests and unbelievable

125

mountains, that I am thoroughly out of tune with trolleys and store clothes and haircuts, and will even be glad of *one* or *two* ticks to remind me of Mother Nature again. . . .[46]

The field work at Tampico that Fuertes was so eagerly anticipating proved every bit as productive as that in the mountains. "Each day brought new wonders," he recalled, listing the dozens of exotic species he observed and collected there.[47] It also brought a new species of oriole, subsequently named *Icterus fuertesi* by Frank Chapman in honor of the man who discovered it.[48]

Common Potoo
Nyctibius griseus
Pencil studies, 9¾″ × 8″
(at left)
Watercolor, 20″ × 13¾″

The trip's primary purpose, as with the other Museum of Natural History expeditions in which Fuertes participated, was to collect specimens and field notes to aid in the construction of a habitat group for the museum. On his return to New York from each trip, Chapman would turn Fuertes' sketches over to Charles Hittell, Hobart Nichols, Carl Rungius, or Bruce Horsfall of the museum staff to work into mural-size landscapes. Fuertes would then be asked to paint specific birds into the background before the mounted specimens and vegetation were installed. The arrangement seems to have been a successful one, and the beautiful dioramas that resulted are still enjoyed by millions of museum visitors.

COLOMBIA—1911

In his autobiographical book, *My Tropical Air Castle,* Frank Chapman explained that his love for the tropics dated from his childhood readings of Amazonian exploration. "We all have our 'Castles in the Air'," he wrote, "but few of us, to use Thoreau's words, succeed in putting 'the foundation under them.' Ever since, as a boy, I read Bates' *Naturalist on the Amazon* and Wallace's *Travels in the Malay Archipelago,* my castle has been in the tropics."[49] After one trip to Mexico and two to Colombia, Fuertes was inclined to agree:

Turquoise-browed Motmot
Eumomota superciliosa
Watercolor
9″ × 11¼″

Gray-breasted Mountain Toucan
Andigena hyoglauca
Watercolor
9½" × 13½"
Colombia, 1912

Tropical longings . . . are, I fancy, a sort of atavism with me. I feel so damn natural when I'm in 'em, and the remembered smell of the first land-whiff, [and] the first roar of the surf on coral reefs . . . all sort of boil up in me every once in a while, and I look out at an approaching winter and remember how easily one slips out—for a time—of all these contacts and gets steeped in the romance and delight of new-old scenes, and hunting and working in all the enthusiasm of discovery.[50]

The museum's 1911 Colombian expedition shipped out of New York on March 13 and arrived in Buenaventura just two weeks later. The party, consisting of Chapman, Fuertes, and a young collector named Leo Miller, was joined there by ornithologist William Richardson (also of the museum staff) before taking a train inland along the Dagua River to Cisneros. Proceeding by mule past Caldas and San Antonio, they arrived in Cali, which was to serve as their base while in the Cauca Valley. "Cali, itself, is the most individual and unspoiled place I ever saw," wrote Fuertes. "There is not a thing in it that has come less than two (and from there up to twenty) days on mule-back, and the people in it look on all the world as outlandish, and tolerate us as being harmlessly imbecile and good pay."[51]

After a day of rest and reorganization, the men returned twelve miles over the preceding day's route and moved into a rented villa some forty miles from the mountains which Chapman had selected as the appropriate background for the museum's diorama display.

Fuertes found the location ideal, with "surpassingly wonderful" views and surprisingly "free from all kinds of bothersome bugs."

129

Chestnut-eared Aracari
Pteroglossus castanotis
Watercolor
11″ × 15″
Colombia, 1913

. . . The forests are gloriously rank and riotous. Leaves as big as our dining table hang from the moss-embedded tree trunks; masses of scarlet flowers tip the ends of vines that fall from the treetops; queer human whistles mingle with whoops and hermit-thrush songs, and owl-like hoots with the thrilling buzz of a gorgeous hummer [hummingbird] as he shoots past. . . .[52]

At the end of a busy week, Fuertes reported:

I'm now about through with my part of the [habitat] group work: I have painted and checked up the study for the background, and made notes of forest-colors for Horsfall to use, and done a lot of flowers, etc., and have also, in the week we've been here, put up about fifty-five or sixty birds, including several doves and trogons which are possessed of tissue-paper skins in which the feathers just stick by special favor of heaven.[53]

Their work finished at San Antonio, the group traveled east, by way of Cali, across the Cauca River Valley to a sugar plantation near Palmira. "The ride across the valley was hot," recalled Fuertes, "but the most thrillingly interesting day's ride I think I ever took, with the green valley, bamboo forests, strange and numerous birds, miles of immense locusts, like the plague of Egypt . . . that nearly obscured the mountains behind. . . ."[54] From

130

"La Manuelita," the ranch in which they were living, the group fanned out for a week's collecting, then moved higher into the mountains to another ranch called "Milaflores."

Frank Chapman considered the forest there the finest of its kind he had ever seen. Fuertes found its immensity overwhelming:

> When it is clear in the woods, the mass of greenery, and the immensity of things, both in size and variety, is sort of stupefying, and you just feel damned small and insignificant and worm-like, and have a strong tendency to whisper instead of talk out loud, but when it is foggy . . . all the infinitely complicated background is lost in gray, and you get the most beautiful silhouettes of enormous trees, isolated more or less from the great forest mass, and see the wonderful grace and form-beauty of the host-tree and all its beautiful parisitic decoration. The whole stem of the tree becomes a great fernery, for a starter, and then wonderfully beautiful great tropical lilies send out gracefully curved stems with 'elephant ear' leaves; pineapple-like plants grow in flowering masses from the joints of the limbs, perpendicular wood-ropes, trimmed with hanging gardens, come from the distant tree-tops, and root in the ground, and a little distance away the theme is repeated, with variations, one shade less green and one shade paler in the gray of the mist. These things make me itch to paint them, but they are in themselves unpaintable, I suppose, and must be enjoyed, like sunsets and opals, only in themselves, and cannot be perpetuated. Which may be a good thing, but it makes me feel very ungenerous to be here hogging all this beauty and excitement, without being able to save it for the rest of you.[55]

Fuertes' letters from the field were often illustrated with quick pen-and-ink sketches. This one from Colombia shows the artist and a friend taking shelter from the rain under a natural umbrella.

Tarantula
Watercolor and pencil
14″ × 9½″
Colombia, 1911

Adding to the beauty of the forest was a wide variety of birds and insects as Fuertes explained:

The birds here are fine—many kinds—probably at least twenty—of hummers, four of parrots, at least three of beautiful trogons, four of toucans, and any number of strange small birds, with queer noises and songs. Of course the insects are wonderful; all kinds of queer, enormous beetles, gigantic spiders and tarantulas, etc., etc., and butterflies beautiful beyond description. The forests are clothed in moss, out of clumps of which grow wonderful orchids, air plants of all kinds, and all hung together by a network of vines and 'wood-ropes.' Gorgeous green and scarlet trogons glide and swoop through them, and parrots yell up in the lighted tree-tops, but on the ground it is nearly dark, and queer little birds run around among the ground plants, never taking wing, but calling like rails, almost under foot but never visible. Some of the very most common have not yet once been seen, though the forest rings with their whistles, and we can at any time call up two or three to within a few feet of us. Curiously silent motmots glide up from near the ground and sit motionless on the vines, while way up in the distant tree-tops giant orioles, like the big one I brought from Mexico, bark, scream, and hoot, up-side-down, and crackle their bills.[56]

132

California Condor, *Gymnogyps californianus*, Wash, 11¾″ × 8¾″

Wattled Jacana, *Jacana jacana,* Wash–and–pencil studies, 13¾″ × 9½″, Colombia, 1911

By mid-May, their collecting completed at "Miraflores," the party returned to Cali through storm-swollen rivers and across "unspeakable roads." From there, Chapman and Fuertes traveled by boat to Cartago, crossed the Andes at the 11,200-foot Quindio Pass, and resumed their river travel at Honda. "Howling monkeys and blue and yellow macaws" cried from the shore, while herons, ibises, and Jabiru storks flew overhead. It was a send-off that made Fuertes eager to return.

COLOMBIA—1913

Fuertes made his second and last trip to Colombia in 1913, again under the auspices of the American Museum of Natural History. The collecting locale, near Bogotá, was to the north and east of the area covered on the 1911 expedition. So this time, Fuertes, Chapman and the four other members of the party entered Columbia directly form the Atlantic. Arriving at Barranquilla by steamer in mid-January, they traveled up the Magdalena River by barge, collecting as they went. "I don't suppose there's a river in the world where there's more to see than on the Magdalena . . ." wrote Fuertes. "Daily, we see both the red and blue and yellow macaws. Big wood ibis, herons, horned screamers, and other striking birds are almost always in sight, and divide the interest with the capybaras (the biggest living rodent —about like a pig) and the crocodiles. . . ."[57]

Colombian landscape
Watercolor
12¼" × 18½"

"Pavo"

Brush Guan.

Crested Guan
Penelope purpurascens
Watercolor
9½″ × 13½″
Colombia, 1911

Of the six members of the expedition, only three—Chapman, Fuertes, and George K. Cherrie—had previous field experience. The other three—Paul Howes, Thomas Ring, and Geoffrey O'Connell—were young men on their first museum collecting trip. Three weeks after their departure from New York, Fuertes was happy to report that the group was getting along well and that the young members were "all eager and good workers" and that the party as a whole was "a particularly congenial crowd."

> The gang is perfectly solid, everybody getting really attached to the others, and the age-lines, I am happy to say, are not drawn at all except as to the matter of authority. Tom is a good-natured guy, funny as he can be, and a most naive and genuine little scout, whom everybody likes. . . . Jeff is an earnest and modest boy, with great possibilities. . . . Paul is quite a good painter, and has a full kit of oils along, and has already done some very creditable little studies. . . . Everybody is absolutely game and there's not any shirk anywhere in the bunch. The real bad thing in such a crowd is a lazy man—and we've no such.[58]

Coming ashore at La Dorada, the party acquired the necessary mules and traveled on to Honda, a town familiar to Fuertes and Chapman from their last visit. From there, three of the party took an important side trip before moving on to Facatativá and finally, by train, to Bogotá. Fuertes explained his productive excursion from Honda:

> Frank and I and Paul Howes, who paints a bit, went up, not to El Alto de Sargento as planned, but to El Consuelo, only five hours away, where there's a

136

superb view. . . . We had marvelous weather, and I painted three big panels showing the whole panorama—a perfect whiz of a view. The painting hours were from 6 a.m. (just light) to from 8 to 10, varying with the day. We only had three mornings, so we did well. F.M.C. is very happy with the pictures, and thinks 'em the best I've done and quite sufficient, so I am also relieved. . . . We feel we have done mighty well, for we have got the great thing we came for—the painting. I feel I have justified my coming, and we have got together about 600 birds as a by-product, and are just starting in.[59]

By the time the party reached Bogotá, several of them, including Fuertes and Howes, had become ill, Fuertes with a three-day fever and Howes with a more serious one. Had it happened anywhere else on their trip, the consequences might have been worse, but in Bogotá they were fortunate in having the help of the American ambassador and a doctor "with a Harvard training and Bellevue Hospital experience."[60]

Leaving Howes behind in case of recurrence of his intermittent fever, the rest of the group fanned out into the nearby mountains to collect samples of local bird life. Compared to the collecting areas of their earlier Colombian

South American Turkey Vulture

Honda, Col. SA
May 28, 1911

South American
Turkey Vulture
Watercolor
14½" × 9½"
Colombia, 1911

trip, Chapman and Fuertes found the Bogotá area somewhat disappointing. "Four weeks more to work in," Fuertes noted in late February:

> Got to do some collecting, and what's more, find some country, if the trip is to pan out anything like the last one. The eastern slopes are barren, treeless, hopeless, sad—and gosh how steep! For days and days, coming this journey, we've gone along little scratches on the mountains' flanks, where turkey buzzards looked like flies above us, and like other flies right straight below us. Such mountains I have never seen. Down, 2,000 or 3,000 feet so nearly under you, as you look off your sleepy ambling mule, that it makes even me gag to do it, a big river, roaring and white, lies as silent and characterless as a kink of thread on the carpet. The brown, wrinkled shoulders of the upper slopes rise, rise—get distantly green where the everlasting clouds hang and make the lofty fog-forest. Along the trails rare little farms, built so steep that they look like maps of farms tacked on the walls, harbor and faintly nourish a scattered people; the poorest, in every conceivable sense, I think, in the world. . . .[61]

The terrain at Buena Vista, south and east of Bogotá, proved much richer in plant and bird life. The forests, all in the Orinoco drainage basin, combined several life zones, making their study particularly rewarding. Fuertes described them as "superb" and "miraculously beautiful":

> There is a June-like climate, no mosquitoes nor flies, no dripping burning perspiration, just cool lovely pestless collecting in enormous dry-floored forest. . . . Perfectly ideal collecting, in the richest fauna I have ever seen, and to me, all new.[62]

Contrary to Fuertes' early fears, the expedition produced an abundance of new specimens. By the time they left Colombia at the end of April, retracing their arrival route, the party had collected more than twenty-four hundred bird specimens, four-hundred of which Fuertes had gathered and would, by agreement with Chapman, retain for his own paintings.

Of the many tricks Fuertes used to attract birds for observation and collection, the most effective was voice mimicry, at which he was unusually gifted. Even when birds were hidden by the lush foliage of the tropics, Fuertes could call them into view with a brief rendition of their song. He employed this technique so successfully in Colombia, with tiny "shadow birds" (antpittas) like the *Grallaria*, that Chapman asked him to prepare a series of papers on "Impressions of the Voices of Tropical Birds" for publication in *Bird-Lore* (1913–1914). Wilfred Osgood of the Field Museum later described the series as "a charming and valuable contribution to a little known subject," and "his most important written work."[63] In 1915 it was reprinted in the Smithsonian Institution's *Annual Report*.

With the outbreak of World War I, there was a decline in the amount of money available for natural history research and publication, and Fuertes' painting commissions came less frequently. Too old for enlistment in the armed forces, Fuertes involved himself with the war effort on the local front

Crescent-faced Antpitta
Grallaricula lineifrons
Pencil study
8½" × 8"
Colombia

by providing artwork for war-related posters and working with the Boy Scouts. "Just now I'm giving the best I can to my scouts," he wrote Chapman in the fall of 1918. "The troop has already coralled over $100,000 in W.S.S. and 3rd Liberty Loan sales, so it isn't a waste of time. . . ."[64]

As the war came to a close, Fuertes' commissions increased and his travel schedule filled out, but it was not until 1926 that he returned to the field as part of a large-scale, fully financed museum expedition.

ABYSSINIA—1926–1927

In the early spring of 1926, Louis Fuertes received a direct and rather startling letter from James E. Baum, a wealthy Chicago writer and sportsman whom

139

California Quail, *Lophortyx californicus,* Watercolor, 15″ × 11″

he had met while vacationing at a Wyoming ranch the summer before. The letter read, in part, as follows:

Crane Lake,
Saskatchewan
Watercolor
7¼″ × 10¾″
1907

> If a man should come to you and ask: 'What is the strangest country in the world to-day? Where is the bird life the most curious and plentiful?' You would unquestionably answer both by one word—Abyssinia.
> All right. Now that we have established the desirability of your going there, what do you say to going with me next September?[65]

Baum went on to explain that he was planning to take his family to Europe, spend the summer in France and England, then embark on a three-month hunting trip in Abyssinia (now Ethiopia). While Fuertes was excited by the idea of seeing Africa, he had some doubts about mixing a working expedition of the sort he would have wished with the recreational expedition Baum was proposing.

On a trip to Chicago a few weeks after receipt of the letter, Fuertes went with Baum to discuss the idea with Wilfred Osgood, curator of zoology at the Field Museum of Natural History and a long-time friend of Fuertes. Osgood became interested in the project, and together they devised a plan whereby the expedition could be officially sanctioned—and financed—by the museum. A week later, Baum talked with his friend Walter Strong,

141

editor of the *Chicago Daily News*, to see if the paper would provide partial support of the expedition in exchange for exclusive rights to cover the trip. At the same time, Osgood approached the museum's president, Stanley Field, and its director, David Charles Davies, to discuss how much of the cost the museum would be willing to underwrite. "We've sold our proposition," wrote Osgood to Fuertes a few days later. "In fact, we're oversubscribed and the privilege of backing us was near to becoming a matter of contention between bidders."[66] Before Osgood's letter arrived, however, the bidding war was over and the results announced: "EVERYTHING ARRANGED—STOP—NEWS WILL FINANCE WHOLE EXPEDITION TO THE EXTENT OF TWENTY-FIVE THOUSAND. HOORAY—JACK BAUM."[67]

The speed with which the trip had been arranged, and the telegram announcing its final settlement, seemed to Fuertes almost too good to be true. "The actuality has always hitherto seemed somewhat nebulous and third-personal," he wrote to Osgood. "Now it looms and it behooves me to assail my job with a purposeful finality it isn't used to!"[68]

The Field Museum/Chicago Daily News Abyssinian Expedition traveled by boat from Marseilles, through the Suez Canal and down the Red Sea,

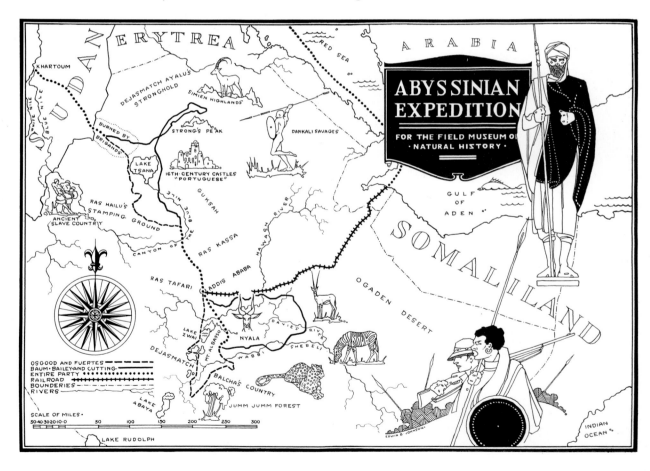

Greater Flamingo
Phoenicopterus ruber
Watercolor study
17″ × 10½″
Abyssinia, 1927

Francolinus clappei

Metemma
April 16 1927

Clapperton's Francolin, *Francolinus clappertoni,* Watercolor study, 12¾″ × 9¾″, Abyssinia, 1927

arriving in Djibouti, French Somaliland, on October 4, 1926. From there, the group traveled three days by train to Addis Ababa, the capital of Abyssinia, 500 miles to the west. In addition to Baum, Fuertes, and Osgood, the party included C. Suydam Cutting—a patron of the Field Museum who had volunteered for the expedition—and Alfred M. Bailey, a young zoologist who had recently joined the museum staff.

"There is no describing Addis," wrote Fuertes a day after arriving in the capital, "so I'll try! Crowded aimless streets—full of people of all sorts, cattle, sheep, goats, camels, horses, burros, and more of the same."[69] To Baum it was a "forest town" surrounded by dense strands of eucalyptus and footpaths winding "everywhere through the woods without apparent rime or reason."[70] And to Bailey, Addis Ababa was "a primitive town, a page turned back to the days of the Arabian Knights."[71]

Taking up residence in the commodious Imperial Hotel, the party spent several weeks purchasing mules, hiring bearers, and obtaining the necessary travel permits. This last important task required an audience with Ras Tafari (Haile Selassie), emperor of Ethiopia. The thirty-four-year-old monarch, whose titles also included Prince Regent, King of Kings, and Conquering Lion of Judah, received the Americans with cordial dignity just a few days after their arrival. "I suppose we were there half an hour," recalled Fuertes:

> After outlining the plans roughly, O[sgood] explained the purposes of our work and presented the two books of photos of the museum and Chicago, and I gave my two books [specially bound copies of the *National Geographic Book of Birds* and *Book of Animals* illustrated by Fuertes] with the request that one be passed on to the Empress. O said, 'These are not expensive gifts; merely evidences of our gratitude, and an explication of the nature of our work.' Ras Tafari then smiled his nicest (which is very nice) and said, 'The thought ahead is worth a great price.' . . . Then, after all business was concluded, the Ras said, 'I will see you again before you leave,' and soon after, we came away. We felt that if we had impressed him as strongly as he did us we should have no trouble.[72]

As Fuertes had hoped, the positive impressions were mutual, and Ras Tafari provided the travel documents necessary to guarantee safe passage for the expedition members to all parts of the country. Before their departure from Addis Ababa, the Ras invited the Americans to an elaborate dinner party with bountiful and delicious food, solid gold dinner service, cut-glass goblets, and china bearing the Abyssinian royal crest. Afterwards, Osgood showed movies of life in America, and discussed the purpose and contents of the Field Museum. "'Why, these animals stand exactly as if they were alive.'" exclaimed the Ras when he saw pictures of the museum's African dioramas. "'I don't understand how stuffed skins can be made to appear so lifelike. Now I can see why people are interested in museums. This is great work you are doing, educational and instructive and I shall be glad to give you every assistance.'"[73]

145

While Ras Tafari's support was the most critical for the expedition's success, offers of assistance from other sources were also accepted with enthusiasm. When a European resident of the capital, Colonel D.A. Sanford, offered the use of his ranch on the rim of the Muger River, thirty miles north of Addis Ababa, Osgood suggested that Fuertes and Bailey accept the invitation.

Traveling first by car, then on horseback, the two men observed an abundance of bird life along the way. "This is the highlight of my ornithological career," exclaimed Fuertes at one point during the trip. "Birds everywhere and every damned one is new to me."[74]

Fuertes' productivity in Abyssinia, both in specimen preparation and painting, is quite remarkable, considering that all of his luggage was lost in transit. In a letter describing the bad luck, he admitted, "I am handicapped by having to use untried and unaccustomed tools, inadequate clothes for the uplands where it gets really cold, no painting or even drawing things at all, and the loss of a whole trunkful of conveniences—drying trays, skinning

Abyssinian Ground Hornbill
Bucorvus abyssinicus
Watercolor study
11¾" × 16½"
Abyssinia, 1927

Narina Trogan, *Apaloderma narina,* Watercolor study, 12¾″ × 10⅜″, Abyssinia, 1926

White-headed Vulture
Trigonoceps occipitalis
Watercolor study
12¾″ × 10¾″
Abyssinia, 1926

tools, etc., that I had carefully planned. . . . But I can get along," he declared, "and it would take a lot more than that to throw me."[75] Borrowing clothing, guns, and skinning supplies from other members of the expedition, and purchasing a small watercolor set in Addis before leaving for the ranch, the ingenious naturalist proceeded through the rest of his Abyssinian stay undaunted.

Colonel Sanford's ranch proved to be almost as exotic as the bird life. Perched on the rim of the Muger Canyon, it overlooked some of the most spectacular scenery in East Africa. "Roses and snapdragons bloomed profusely, and the view from the front porch across the rose-filled garden and the deep canyon beyond was one we were not likely to forget," recalled Bailey.[76] Since the two men had the ranch to themselves, with a full staff of servants to support them, their work was not inhibited by social obligations.

148

Rising at dawn, each would spend the morning collecting—Fuertes, birds; and Bailey, small mammals. By 9:30 or 10:00, they would return to the house for a day's worth of specimen preparation. "We sit on the porch skinning," wrote Fuertes, "and toss the bodies of birds and mice into the air; none has yet hit ground, for a dozen graceful kites sailing around nip them on the fly as daintily as can be."[77]

Fuertes and Bailey were sorry to leave the ranch after only six days, but when Osgood wrote that preparations for the expedition's southern trip to Arusi had been completed and the rest of the party would soon be ready to depart, they had little choice but to return to Addis Ababa. Each had prepared over eighty specimens for the museum during their stay at the Muger Canyon.

On October 30, 1926, almost a month after its arrival in Addis Ababa, the expedition was ready to leave for Arusi. "It was like setting off to the wars this afternoon," wrote Jack Baum in his first syndicated column about the expedition:

> A string of thirty-six pack mules makes an imposing outfit. Add to that, nine mounted men, nagahdis, personal boys, two cooks and two interpreters. Those men must ride. They are not to be confused with the twenty common packers or muleteers who walk. . . . Strung out along the line carrying their old-style French army guns, model 1870, were ten sabanias, or guards . . . with heavy cartridge belts gleaming in the bright sunlight. . . . We forded a stream, climbed a long sloping hill and saw before us Mount Zuquala, rising like a gigantic pyramid to the south. The broad African landscape spread out at our feet with its thornbush, its flat-topped acacia trees, its shimmering haze, its illimitable distances, its broad plains. That trying six months of preparation was over. The trip had begun.[78]

Letters from Abyssinia in which Fuertes describes the party's pet baboon, Tinish.

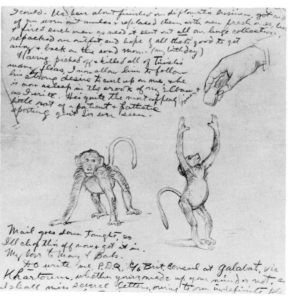

Gelada Baboons at Muger Canyon, *Papio gelada*, Watercolor, 12¾″ × 10″, Abyssinia, 1926

Wattled Plover
Vanellus senegallus
Watercolor study
14″ × 10″
Abyssinia, 1927

By the time they returned to Addis Ababa two months later, the expedition had succeeded in one of its missions: obtaining specimens of the beautiful horned nyala for a habitat group in the Field Museum. Fuertes and Osgood, who had split off from the rest of the group, had collected over an extensive area to the south. Fuertes reported in a letter to his wife that during

151

Abyssinian Black-and-white Colobus
Colobus abyssinicus
Pencil studies
10¾″ × 12½″
Abyssinia, 1927

Near Alata
Sidamo—
Dec 15 - 1926—
Bycanistes cristatus - ♂.

the course of the trip he had "painted 50 or 60 field studies, many quite elaborate, and collected and preserved 559 birds . . . in over 40 different camps."[79] Osgood, who had been collecting with Fuertes, returned with nearly 500 mammal specimens, including a number of large antelope.

At their reunion in the capital city in late January, the two exploring parties had many tales of adventure to relate. Encounters with wandering bands of brigand "shiftas" and a near-fatal leopard attack had added excitement to the Baum, Bailey, and Cutting party's experiences. Osgood and Fuertes found their adventures somewhat less dangerous, except for one occasion when Fuertes, separated from the main caravan, was hailed and held "social prisoner" by a local chieftain for more than two hours. "We had, of course, many picturesque experiences," recounted Fuertes, "my top-notcher, perhaps, being a late afternoon swim in Lake Sh'ala with the hippopotami coming up to huffle and blow every few minutes, often quite near by. They were not at all alarmed, and we had a very nice swim together!"[80]

Silvery-cheeked Hornbill
Bycanistes brevis
Watercolor study
10¾" × 12¾"
Abyssinia, 1926

153

20 Miles North-west
of Lake Tsana.
—April 6, 1927—

Hoopoe

Upupa epops —

Hoopoe
Upupa epops
Watercolor study
12¾″ × 9⅝″
Abyssinia, 1927

During their second stay in Addis Ababa, the Field Museum party was again entertained by Haile Selassie, who took a keen interest in their travels and scientific work. When Fuertes showed him some of the bird studies he had made in the field, wrote Jack Baum, "The Ras was much impressed, especially by one of a guinea fowl, so much so, in fact, that he ordered an attendant to bring in a live guinea fowl. He compared the live bird to the picture and gasped at the resemblance. . . ."[81] Fuertes asked the Ras to choose one of the studies he liked, to be worked up into a finished painting by which he could remember the expedition. The Ras chose a trogon.

After replenishing supplies in Addis Ababa and bidding farewell to the emperor, the expedition headed north toward the mountainous province of

154

Gojam. They camped on the 10,000-foot summit of Mount Entoto, then at Colonel Sanford's ranch on the Muger River, where Fuertes and Bailey had made their first Abyssinian collections.

After a study of the canyon bottom, not previously visited, the caravan traveled further north and entered a large plateau, an agricultural area "tilled by strong-looking Gallas who drove oxen hitched to plows which were merely crooked sticks."[82] From there, the party descended into the deep chasm of the Abbai River, or Blue Nile, and after an arduous climb up the far side, arrived in Gojam, a province governed by the powerful Ras Hailu. There they were met by a messenger with greetings from the Ras and an invitation to visit in the provincial capital, Bichana. "Our reception by the great chieftain was all that anyone could ask," recalled Bailey:

> Our caravan of approximately a hundred mules crossed a weak bridge over the river without any of the heavily laden animals falling through. We finally came to a high ridge. We climbed the steep hill and were amazed to see an assemblage of half a thousand soldiers sent out to greet us. It was a touch of the Arabian Knights and medieval splendor; the white-clad Abyssinians headed by a dignified chamberlain were drawn up in double file, and a reed-and-trumpet band blew lustily on their instruments—each one capable of playing a single note. We made a triumphant march across the plains, preceded by the band and followed by the throng of soldiers. A large tent had been erected for us. The ground was covered with oriental rugs, and we made ourselves comfortable while lunch was being prepared. Greetings were sent to the Ras, and it was not long before lines of slaves were before our tent bearing gifts of tej (a native mead), beer, chickens and eggs, and an ox to be killed for our men.[83]

Fuertes with
Fitaurari Adamassu,
a local chief in Gojam,
northern Abyssinia, 1927.

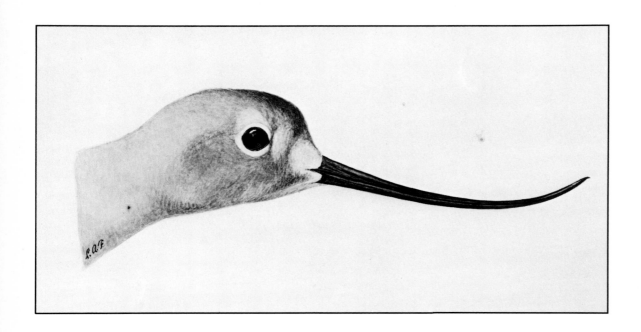

American Avocet
Recurvirostra americana
Wash
5½″ × 9¾″

After several days of feasting and entertainment, and a hunt with the Ras at which a thousand of his followers were in attendance, the party left Bichana.

As before, the expedition divided into two groups. Baum, Bailey, and Cutting went north to the Simyen Highlands to collect Abyssinian ibex and other big game. Fuertes and Osgood traveled west of Lake Tsana in search of birds and small mammals.

Along the trail, Fuertes spotted a large snake in the trail ahead of his party. Since few snakes had been collected during the expedition, he drew his revolver and shot the six-foot reptile from the saddle. Then, according to Bailey, he dismounted and "in spite of the horrified protests of the natives, he picked it up. He was careless; the snake was not dead, and it struck, just scraping the skin of his hand."[84] Months later, Osgood wrote from the Field Museum to tell Fuertes that the snake had been identified as a Mamba, probably the most poisonous species in Africa. "Maybe there is a God, after all," wrote Osgood, recalling his friend's close call.[85]

The divided parties met as planned after two months' separation and, traveling together through dangerous brigand country, crossed the Sudanese border and arrived in Khartoum on May 1st. There, Bailey recorded in his journal, the party "stayed at the Grant Hotel, a rambling first-class affair on the banks of the Blue Nile," where they attended to the packing of their specimens. "A carpenter was hired and 22 cases of specimens, etc., were packed."[86] Fuertes wrote his son Sumner that the trip had provided "a lot of fun and interest" and had "netted 2,000 birds, 1,400 mammals and 100 'scattering' specimens—3,500 in all, all first class and of very valuable stuff."[87]

156

Malachite Kingfisher, *Alcedo cristata*, Watercolor study, 12½″ × 9¾″, Abyssinia, 1927

Anubis Baboon
Papio anubis
Pencil study
10¾″ × 12¾″
Abyssinia, 1926

After a week in Khartoum, the expedition steamed up the Nile and, after stops in Cairo and Alexandria, crossed the Mediterranean, which Bailey and the others found "delightfully cool . . . in contrast to the 115 degrees we had experienced in the Sudan."[88]

Meeting his wife and daughter in London, Fuertes returned to the United States with them in May. As their boat headed for New York, another American was making history in the air above them. Though they did not see his plane, the Fuertes delighted in the news of Charles Lindbergh's successful trans-Atlantic flight.

The Abyssinian trip, Fuertes' longest and most distant, was also his last, for less than three months after his return he suffered the fatal automobile accident that left his friends and admirers stunned and saddened. In a *Bird-*

158

Hooded Merganser, *Lophodytes cucullatus,* Ink wash, 9½″ × 8½″

Egyptian Vulture, *Neophron percnopterus,* Watercolor study, 16″ × 10⅝″, Abyssinia, 1927

Lore obituary, Frank Chapman commented on Fuertes' qualities as a field naturalist and on his value as a friend:

> Fuertes' value in the field was not restricted to his cheerful comradeship and his skill as an artist. He was a keen, tireless, and persistent collector and a stimulating scientific associate. In the Canadian Rockies it was Fuertes who discovered the nests of Ptarmigan and Pipit that appear in the American Museum's Arctic-Alpine Group. In Mexico it was Fuertes who in the field recognized as new the Oriole subsequently named for him, and in the dense subtropical forests of the Colombian Andes he secured specimens and identified the notes of birds which no other member of our party saw.

> Nor did he confine his activities to science and art, to preserving birds as well as to painting them. Always he did more than his share of the work incident to travel and life in the open. He was an experienced woodsman, a good packer, a capital cook, a master hand with tools, who could mend anything, and in adversity and sickness no mother could have been more tender.

> So one might continue to enumerate the qualities for which Fuertes was beloved and still fail to convey a realization of the rare personal charm which made his mere presence a source of joyous possibilities. To those who lives were enriched by his friendship the world will never be the same again.[89]

Title page design for *Bird-Lore* with Red Crossbills
Loxia curvirostra
Watercolor and ink
9¼" × 13½"

Louis Agassiz Fuertes—Chronology

1874		Louis Agassiz Fuertes (LAF) born February 7 in Ithaca, New York, the son of Mary Perry of Troy, New York, and Estevan Antonio Fuertes of Puerto Rico.
1888		LAF makes his first painting from life, a male red crossbill.
1892	*August*	LAF travels with his family to Paris, studying there and in Switzerland through the winter of 1893. He works with the staff of the natural history museum in Zurich, increasing his knowledge of birds and other areas of natural history.
1893	*September*	Returning to Ithaca, LAF enters Cornell University as a freshman with plans to major in engineering.
1894	*December*	LAF meets Elliott Coues, the country's leading ornithologist, during a Cornell University Glee Club trip to Washington, D.C.
1895	*Summer*	LAF travels to Europe with the Cornell Glee Club. In his free time, he sketches animals in European zoos.
	November	Elliott Coues exhibits LAF's paintings at the American Ornithologists' Union Congress in Washington, D.C. LAF receives his first commissions for book illustrations.
1896	*September*	LAF begins work on 111 illustrations for *Citizen Bird* by Elliott Coues and Mabel Osgood Wright. The project is completed before his graduation the following spring.
	November	Elliott Coues introduces LAF to the scientific community at the American Ornithologists' Union annual congress in Cambridge, Massachusetts. LAF meets many of those who will play important roles in his career, including Frank M. Chapman, Edward Howe Forbush, C. Hart Merriam, and Abbott Thayer.
1897	*June*	LAF graduates from Cornell University with a B.A. His senior thesis is on the coloration of birds.
	Summer	LAF spends the summer in Dublin, New Hampshire, receiving instruction in painting and observation of color and light from Abbott Thayer. He moves to Scarborough, New York, with the Thayer family in September.
1898	*March*	LAF travels to Florida with Abbott Thayer, Gerald Thayer, and Charles Knight. His first full-fledged expedition lasts six weeks.
1899	*January*	LAF is invited to illustrate a new edition of Elliott Coues' *Key to North American Birds.*
	June	LAF joins Edward H. Harriman's privately sponsored scientific expedition to Alaska. The influential group aboard the S.S. *George W. Elder* provides LAF with many lifelong associations.
1901	*April*	LAF begins summer's field research for the United States Biological Survey, joining Vernon Bailey and Harry C. Oberholser in Texas for several months.
	November	LAF elected to membership in the American Ornithologists' Union (AOU).
1902	*April*	LAF departs on American Museum of Natural History expedition to the Bahamas, led by Frank M. Chapman.

1903	*June*	LAF takes AOU trip to California, Nevada, New Mexico, and Colorado with Frank M. Chapman.
1904	*June*	LAF marries Margaret Sumner; the couple takes a wedding trip to Jamaica, where the honeymoon becomes a collecting expedition.
	November	LAF works on background painting for the flamingo habitat group at the American Museum of Natural History. It is the first of many museum dioramas that he will create.
1907	*June*	LAF joins Frank M. Chapman on an AOU bird trip to Saskatchewan and Alberta.
1908	*April*	LAF joins Frank M. Chapman and Arthur Cleveland Bent for an American Museum of Natural History expedition to the Cuthbert Rookery in southern Florida.
1909	*August*	LAF participates in American Museum of Natural History collecting trip to the Magdalen Islands in the Gulf of St. Lawrence.
1910	*April*	LAF departs for a Museum of Natural History collecting trip to the Yucatan, led by Frank M. Chapman.
		Birds of New York, a comprehensive two-volume work written by Elon Howard Eaton and illustrated with more than one hundred color plates by LAF, is published.
1911	*March*	LAF joins Frank M. Chapman and others for a three-month expedition in Colombia on behalf of the Museum of Natural History.
1913	*January*	LAF participates in a second Museum of Natural History expedition to Colombia, returning to Ithaca in April.

Fuertes, president of the Cayuga Bird Club, addresses school children and their parents on a bird walk near Ithaca.

1916	*Summer*	LAF works on a major National Geographic commission to illustrate "The Larger North American Mammals" (published in November). It is the first of three mammal series he will paint for the magazine.
	July	George Miksch Sutton visits Fuertes' family at Sheldrake Point to study painting under the direction of LAF.
1920	*May*	LAF makes a second trip to the Bahamas to study flamingos for his mural commission at the Flamingo Hotel in Miami Beach, Florida.
1920	*November*	LAF meets Allan Brooks during an AOU annual congress in Washington, D.C. The two artists become close friends and collaborators on several important book projects.
1921	*January*	LAF and Allan Brooks travel to Florida together to observe and paint birds.
1922		LAF enters contract with Edward Howe Forbush and the Commonwealth of Massachusetts over color plates for *Birds of Massachusetts and Other New England States*. He will work on the commission until his death in 1927.
	November	LAF is appointed "resident lecturer" at Cornell—his only official position on the Cornell faculty.
1925		LAF's gorilla sculpture, cast in 1923, is exhibited at the Pennsylvania Academy of the Fine Arts.
1926	*October*	LAF joins expedition to Abyssinia sponsored by the Field Museum of Natural History and the *Chicago Daily News*.
1927	*May*	LAF completes his Abyssinian trip, meets his wife and daughter in Europe, and they return to Ithaca.
	August	LAF is killed at a railroad crossing near Unadilla, New York (August 22).

Fuertes with a live Snowy Owl, *Nyctea scandiaca,* c. 1920.

Major Institutional Collections of Paintings by Louis Agassiz Fuertes

During Louis Agassiz Fuertes' thirty-year professional career (1897–1927), he produced literally thousands of paintings. Working in a wide variety of media—pencil, ink, watercolor, and oils—Fuertes created more bird paintings than any previous artist. While some of that work has been lost with time, a surprising amount of it has survived.

The greatest concentration of Fuertes' originals may be found in the collections of the following eight institutions.

THE ACADEMY OF NATURAL SCIENCES OF PHILADELPHIA

The Academy of Natural Sciences of Philadelphia received the bulk of its Fuertes holdings as part of a long-term renewable loan from the United States Fish and Wildlife Service in 1978. The 220 original watercolors, washes, and ink drawings are all works that were commissioned by the United States Biological Survey and Department of Agriculture between 1899 and 1926.

The collection includes the final paintings from Fuertes' 1901 Texas survey, many of which were never published during Fuertes' lifetime. They were used to illustrate *The Bird Life of Texas* by Harry C. Oberholser, edited by Edgar B. Kincaid, Jr. (Austin: University of Texas Press, 1974).

Another important group of paintings within the collection are Fuertes' "Fifty Common Birds of Farm and Orchard," originally published as a United States Department of Agriculture Farmers' Bulletin, and later republished in the *National Geographic Magazine* in June 1913. In a letter to Fuertes of October 22, 1913, T. S. Palmer of the Biological Survey observed, "Nothing you have ever done has brought your work to the attention of so many readers as the plates in 'Fifty Common Birds.' The various editions now aggregate nearly half a million copies."

While the paintings in the collection represent birds from most of Fuertes' foreign travels—with the exception of Africa—the majority of the works depict North American species. There are also six mammal subjects in the collection.

The Academy's other major Fuertes holdings consist of manuscript materials, primarily in the form of correspondence with Witmer Stone (1866–1939), the Academy's curator of ornithology from 1908 to 1924, and its director from 1924 to 1928. The Fuertes letters in the Stone Collection were written between 1899 and 1926, and cover a great number of topics. A few original sketches are included in this material.

In 1979, with financial support from the Institute for Museum Services, the Academy began an extensive conservation program to preserve the Fuertes watercolors in its collection. Since that time, the Academy has spent $12,000 to remove the fragile paintings from the highly acidic cardboard on which they had been mounted, and to properly mat and store them under acid-free conditions.

Working in cooperation with Olin Library at Cornell University, the Academy is now gathering information for a comprehensive Fuertes catalog, which will individually identify all paintings, washes, and drawings by Louis Agassiz Fuertes housed in public collections.

THE AMERICAN MUSEUM OF NATURAL HISTORY

The American Museum of Natural History owns 403 original drawings and paintings by Louis Agassiz Fuertes, most of which were purchased from Mrs. Fuertes shortly after the artist's death. Dr. Frank M. Chapman, Fuertes' longtime friend and field companion, made the selection in order to represent a cross section of the artist's subjects and styles. For that reason, the collection contains field sketches, preliminary drawings, and final watercolors from every period of Fuertes' life. Paintings made on his various American Museum expeditions or relating to the museum's habitat groups are well represented.

In March 1977, the American Museum received a donation of eighteen early wash drawings from Charles Scribner's Sons. These are the original illustrations for *Song Birds and Water Fowl* by H. E. Parkhurst (New York: Charles Scribner's Sons, 1897).

In addition to its Fuertes paintings, the American Museum cares for an important collection of manuscript materials relating to Fuertes and his work. Of these, the most numerous are letters between Dr. Chapman and the artist, in which expeditions, museum exhibitions, plates for *Bird-Lore,* and other ornithological matters are discussed.

CORNELL UNIVERSITY

Cornell University's collection of Louis Agassiz Fuertes papers and artwork is the most extensive in the United States. It is divided into three principal repositories: Olin Library, the Laboratory of Ornithology, and the Herbert F. Johnson Museum of Art.

Olin Library

The Olin Library's Fuertes collection consists of 7.5 cubic feet of personal papers and photographs, and over one thousand watercolors and studies. This collection, given to the Department of Manuscripts and University Archives by Mary Fuertes Boynton, documents Fuertes' evolving talent and style through both his written words and his artwork.

Fuertes' correspondence with fellow naturalists and artists reveals some of the issues that concerned him in bird painting. A series of letters from Abbott Thayer advises Fuertes on the importance of Thayer's theory of "concealing coloration" and reveals Thayer's influence on Fuertes' work. Letters from Richard E. Bishop, Courtenay Brandreth, Frank M. Chapman, Edward Howe Forbush, Witmer Stone, and George Miksch Sutton discuss birds and ornithological illustration. Nearly five hundred letters, written to Mary Fuertes Boynton after Fuertes' death, describe him and his work. Other written material includes student notes, notebooks, journals and sketchbooks; diaries; journals from expeditions—many illustrated by sketches; notes; and articles and clippings by and about Fuertes.

The photographic prints and negatives in the collection complement the written material in documenting Fuertes' work. Fuertes took over five hundred photographs on expeditions to Mexico, the Yucatan, the Bahamas, Jamaica, Colombia, the Andes, and other South American regions. Other photographic material includes negatives of some sketches and color reproductions of some of his paintings.

The artwork consists of several sketchbooks and over one thousand drawings and watercolors. The bulk of the collection is small pencil, ink, or preliminary watercolors of individual birds or groups of birds, and drawings of specific anatomical details. There are also a few drawings of animals such as rabbits, deer, and apes. Some of the pencil and ink studies are finished works. Included are over two hundred finished watercolors or chalk drawings.

The collection represents every period of Fuertes' development as an artist from his crudest teenage drawings to sketches made during the last year of his life. All of the works are on paper or bristol board. Many of the paper pieces have sketches on both sides of the page, and many sketches include experimental habitat and plumage colors. The works on bristol board are finished pieces, many from Fuertes' early career. A number of pencil sketches pulled from small notebooks and sketchpads are also present.

Several pieces are examples of Fuertes' experimentation with new and different techniques. Among the most interesting are collage/paintings in which Fuertes applied small scraps of paper to watercolors to create a more vivid impression of depth. Fuertes also experimented with painting on photographs of his works, and some examples of this technique are included in the collection.

Laboratory of Ornithology

The Laboratory of Ornithology at Cornell University houses over one hundred watercolors, black-and-white wash drawings, and oil paintings by Fuertes. Most of the collection was donated to the laboratory by Fuertes' family and friends. The pictures illustrate a broad range of subjects, from watercolors of North and Central American bird life, mammals, and fish to portraits of his friends' pets. The watercolors and washes represent the many stages of Fuertes' artistic career, beginning with sketches done at the age of fifteen. This collection also contains some of Fuertes' personal effects, such as his paint boxes, several self-portraits, and a bronze cast of a gorilla.

Of special interest is the laboratory's Fuertes Room. This room is an accurate reconstruction of the study of Frederick Foster Brewster, a friend and great admirer of Fuertes. Set into panels of Java teak are oil paintings depicting waterfowl, game birds, seabirds, and birds of prey. Some are classic interpretations of birds in their environment, while others illustrate Fuertes' experimentation with concealing coloration of birds.

In 1981, the laboratory acquired the Arm and Hammer collection of thirty watercolors of birds of prey, donated by Church and Dwight Co. in Piscataway, New Jersey.

Herbert F. Johnson Museum of Art

The Fuertes collection in the Johnson Museum consists of sixteen watercolors and ink washes, all presented to Cornell University by friends of the artist and members of his family. They range in date from 1899 to approximately 1910. One of the watercolors is clearly a preliminary study for the loon plate in *Birds of New York* (published in 1910), but the rest are finished paintings prepared for gift, sale, or publication. Several date from the artist's 1901 Texas trip.

THE FIELD MUSEUM OF NATURAL HISTORY

The Field Museum Library owns a total of 115 works by Fuertes. One hundred-thirteen of these works were the result of Fuertes' work on the Field Museum/Chicago Daily News Abyssinian Expedition of 1926–1927, and were presented to the museum in October 1927 by C. Suydam Cutting, who accompanied the Expedition.

The works from the Abyssinian Expedition include seventy-six watercolors and thirty-seven pencil drawings. Small pencil sketches also appear on a number of the watercolors. Seventy-two pieces are of ornithological subjects (twelve pencil drawings and sixty watercolors); the remaining forty-one are of other subjects, including twenty-one of primates (principally Gelada baboons and Guereza monkeys), fourteen of other mammals, three of plants, and one of an insect. There is also a pencil sketch of an Ethiopian native and a map of Abyssinia showing the route of the expedition. The majority of these pieces are of a similar size, roughly 11″ × 13″. The rest vary considerably from about 7″ × 9″ to sizes as large as 15″ × 20″.

Thirty-two of the watercolors from this collection were reproduced in the Field Museum's special publication, *Album of Abyssinian Birds and Mammals from Paintings by Louis Agassiz Fuertes* (1930). Wilfred

Hudson Osgood's *Artist and Naturalist in Ethiopia* (1936) includes sixteen of the watercolors reproduced in the *Album,* while Frederick George Marcham's *Louis Agassiz Fuertes and the Singular Beauty of Birds* (1971) includes ten of the watercolors from the *Album,* as well as five other works not previously reproduced. A rendering of the bateleur eagle (No. 12 in the *Album*) also appeared on the dust jacket of Leslie Brown's *African Birds of Prey* (1971).

The library also owns two other watercolors by Fuertes: *Horned Owl* (28″ × 22″), signed and dated 1918; and *Goshawk* (20″ × 30″), signed and dated 1914. How and when the museum acquired these two works is unknown.

COMMONWEALTH OF MASSACHUSETTS

Thirty-three watercolors by Louis Agassiz Fuertes were commissioned by the Commonwealth of Massachusetts to illustrate volume one of Edward Howe Forbush's *Birds of Massachusetts and Other New England States,* published in 1925. Shortly thereafter, the originals were put on long-term loan to the Boston Society of Natural History by the governor and the Massachusetts Department of Agriculture. Subsequently, as a second and third volume were published, additional Fuertes watercolors joined the collection in the same way. By 1930, three years after the artist's death, a total of ninety paintings comprised the collection. These were displayed for many years at the Boston Museum of Science (the museum which grew out of the old Society of Natural History in 1947).

In 1961 the collection was recalled by the commonwealth and is now in the archives of the Secretary's Office.

NATIONAL AUDUBON SOCIETY

During his long and friendly professional relationship with Frank M. Chapman, Louis Agassiz Fuertes painted a large number of plates for reproduction in Chapman's ornithological magazine *Bird-Lore.* Many of the original watercolors and ink washes reproduced in the magazine from 1904 to 1927 are now in the collection of the National Audubon Society. Most represent groups of closely related bird species shown against general habitat backgrounds.

The seventy paintings that comprise the National Audubon Society's Fuertes Collection were used for many years in the traveling "Audubon Art Tours." Since 1979, they have been reproduced, one plate at a time, in the society's publication *American Birds*.

THE NATIONAL GEOGRAPHIC SOCIETY

In June 1913, the *National Geographic Magazine* published in color a group of fifty watercolors by Louis Agassiz Fuertes entitled, "Fifty Common Birds of Farm and Orchard" (the originals were owned by the United States Department of Agriculture and are now on deposit at The Academy of Natural Sciences of Philadelphia). This publication marked the beginning of a long and fruitful relationship between Fuertes and Gilbert Grosvenor, director of the society. By 1920 Fuertes had produced illustrations of "Birds of Town and Country" (May 1914), "American Game Birds" (August 1915), "The Larger North American Mammals" (November 1916), "The Warblers of North America" (April 1917), "The Smaller North American Mammals" (May 1918), "Our Common Dogs" (March 1919), and "Falconry, The Sport of Kings" (December 1920). Many of these illustrations were subsequently used in National Geographic books on the subjects depicted. Although Gilbert Grosvenor invited Fuertes to do additional illustrations of fishes, reptiles, butterflies, and stars, the artist declined invitations in order to accept other painting assignments. The National Geographic Society owns 217 of the original watercolors commissioned for use in its magazine.

NEW YORK STATE MUSEUM, ALBANY

In 1915 a group of 120 watercolors by Louis Agassiz Fuertes was presented to the New York State Museum by Mrs. Russell Sage, a longtime friend of the artist. Representing all the common bird species of New York, the paintings were originally commissioned by the state to illustrate *Birds of New York* by Elon Howard Eaton (volume one, containing plates 1–42, was published in 1910; volume two, with plates 43–106, appeared in 1914). The paintings were subsequently used to illustrate *Birds of America*, edited by T. Gilbert Pearson (The University Society, 1917; New York: Doubleday, 1936).

Although the collection has suffered some mishandling in the past (many of the group paintings were cut apart in preparation for exhibition in 1958), it is now receiving proper curatorial care from the Division of Historical Services section of the museum, to which it was transferred in 1977.

One of Fuertes' bronze gorilla bookends is also included in the museum's collection.

Dovekie
Plautus alle
Wash and
pencil studies
9″ × 7″

List of Illustrations

PICTURE CREDIT KEY

AM:	Photographs by Edward S. Curtis and others, from Harriman Family Archives, courtesy of *Audubon Magazine*.
AMNH:	American Museum of Natural History
ANSP:	The Academy of Natural Sciences of Philadelphia
FMNH:	Field Museum of Natural History
JM/CU:	Herbert F. Johnson Museum of Art/ Cornell University
LO/CU:	Laboratory of Ornithology/Cornell University
NAS:	National Audubon Society
NGS:	National Geographic Society
OL/CU:	Olin Library/Cornell University

Page

i LAF's bookplate; private collection
ii Red-breasted Merganser: AMNH
iv White-breasted Nuthatch: OL/CU
vi Red-headed Woodpecker: ANSP
viii Ocellated Quail: ANSP
xiii Waterfowl in flight: OL/CU
xiv African Fish Eagle: FMNH
2 Harlequin Duck: AMNH
3 Horned Grebe: OL/CU
5 Bobolink: ANSP
6 King Rail: JM/CU
7 Caricature: OL/CU
8 Osprey head: OL/CU
9 Fish drawings: OL/CU
10 *Citizen Bird* plate: ANSP
13 Semipalmated Plover: AMNH
14 The S.S. *George W. Elder*: AM
15 Whip Scorpion: AMNH
17 Zone-tailed Hawk: ANSP
19 Pomarine Jaeger: AMNH
20 Rufous Hummingbird: AMNH
21 LAF in his Ithaca studio: OL/CU
23 Canada Geese: LO/CU
24 Arm and Hammer Baking Soda cards: ANSP
26 White Gyrfalcon: Charles B. Ferguson
29 Chestnut-sided Warbler: OL/CU

30 Bataleur: OL/CU
31 Rose-breasted Grosbeaks: OL/CU
32 Slate-colored Junco: OL/CU
33 House Sparrow with feathers: AMNH
34 Pileated Woodpecker head: AMNH
36 *Citizen Bird* plate: ANSP
37 LAF with Thayer children and friends: OL/CU
38 Pied-billed Grebe: ANSP
40 Tree Sparrow: AMNH
42 White-breasted Nuthatch: AMNH
43 American Anhinga: AMNH
44 LAF, Abbott Thayer et al. in Florida: OL/CU
46 Dead Rabbit studies: OL/CU
48 American Kestrel: ANSP
49 Brewer's Blackbird: ANSP
51 Great Horned Owl: ANSP; Study: OL/CU
53 Three Sparrow heads: OL/CU
54 Common Goldeneye (both): OL/CU
55 Three Sapsuckers: ANSP
57 Harlequin Quail: ANSP; Studies: OL/CU
58 Horned and Tufted Puffins: LO/CU
59 Curlew Sandpiper: Charles B. Ferguson
60 Roadrunner: ANSP; Ink study: AMNH
61 Roadrunner head: AMNH
63 Long-eared Owl: ANSP; Study: OL/CU
64 Greater Earless Lizard: AMNH
65 Great Curassow: ANSP
66 Sharp-shinned Hawk: LO/CU
69 Sora: ANSP; Studies: OL/CU
71 Green Heron: ANSP
72 Blacktail Jackrabbit: ANSP; Study: OL/CU
75 St. Bernard: NGS
76 Ringtail: NGS
77 Five Loons: JM/CU
79 A composition of Owl heads: AMNH
80 Cover for *The Auk*, 1914: ANSP
81 Cover for *The Auk*, 1915: ANSP
83 Peregrine Falcon: Mr. and Mrs. Scott Brooks
84 Elk: LO/CU
85 Passenger Pigeon: OL/CU
86 Lammergeier: FMNH
87 LAF with Lammergeier: LO/CU
87 Lammergeier Studies: FMNH
88 Common Crane: FMNH
89 Mountain Gorilla sculpture (photo): OL/CU

91 Snow Goose and Ring-necked Pheasant: OL/CU

93 Barn Owl: ANSP

95 Eastern Phoebe: ANSP

97 Peregrine Falcon with Green-winged Teal: ANSP

98 Maroon-tailed Parakeet: AMNH

100 Harriman Alaska Expedition route map: AM

101 John Burroughs and John Muir: AM

102 The S.S. *George W. Elder*: AM

103 Common Raven: OL/CU

104 Eskimo craft and *Elder*: AM

105 Long-tailed Jaegers (from the Harriman Alaska Expedition Report): ANSP

106 Harlequin Quail: OL/CU

109 Black Phoebe: ANSP

110 Canyon Wren: JM/CU

111 Bannertail Kangaroo Rat: ANSP

112 Gila Woodpecker: ANSP

113 Greater Antillean Grackle: ANSP

114 Pygmy Nuthatch: JM/CU

115 Streak-backed Oriole: ANSP

117 Short-eared Owl: ANSP; Study: OL/CU

118 LAF with Flamingo aboard the *Estrella*: OL/CU

119 American Flamingo: AMNH

120 Young Cinnamon Teal: AMNH

121 Black-necked Stilt: AMNH

122 Atlantic Puffin: AMNH

123 Burrowing Owl: ANSP

124 LAF with Ptarmigan: AMNH

125 Emerald Toucanet: ANSP

127 Common Potoo: ANSP; Studies: OL/CU

128 Turquoise-browed Motmot: ANSP

129 Gray-breasted Mountain Toucan: OL/CU

130 Chestnut-eared Aracari: AMNH

131 Pen-and-ink sketch from letter: OL/CU

132 Tarantula: OL/CU

133 California Condor: LO/CU

134 Wattled Jacana: AMNH

135 Colombian landscape: AMNH

136 Crested Guan: AMNH

137 Turkey Vulture: AMNH

139 Crescent-faced Antpitta: OL/CU

140 California Quail: ANSP

141 Crane Lake, Saskatchewan: AMNH

142 Map of Field Museum's Abyssinian expedition: *Savage Abyssinia,* James E. Baum

143 Greater Flamingo: FMNH

144 Clapperton's Francolin: FMNH

146 Abyssinian Ground Hornbill: FMNH

147 Narina Trogon: FMNH

148 White-headed Vulture: FMNH

149 Pencil sketch from letter: OL/CU

150 Gelada Baboons at Muger Canyon: FMNH

151 Wattled Plover: FMNH

152 Abyssinian Black-and-white Colobus: FMNH

153 Silvery-cheeked Hornbill: FMNH

154 Hoopoe: FMNH

155 LAF with Fitaurari Adamassu: OL/CU

156 American Avocet head: OL/CU

157 Malachite Kingfisher: FMNH

158 Anubis Baboon: FMNH

159 Hooded Merganser: OL/CU

160 Egyptian Vulture: FMNH

161 Title page design for *Bird-Lore*: OL/CU

163 LAF with schoolchildren: OL/CU

164 LAF with Snowy Owl: OL/CU

168 Dovekie: AMNH

170 LAF Self-caricature: OL/CU

175 Red-breasted Merganser: OL/CU

Self-caricature of Fuertes in the field, from a letter, 1909.

Notes

In the interest of space, the most frequently cited repositories for original manuscript materials have been abbreviated as follows:
ANSP—The Academy of Natural Sciences of Philadelphia
AMNH—American Museum of Natural History
FMNH—Field Museum of Natural History
OL/CU—Olin Library/Cornell University
Because Louis Agassiz Fuertes' name appears in almost every reference, it has been abbreviated as LAF.

PART I

1. Frank M. Chapman, "Fuertes and Audubon," *Natural History*, March 1937.

2. Frank M. Chapman, from remarks made at Fuertes Memorial Service, Cornell University, 30 October 1927, quoted in Mary Fuertes Boynton, *Louis Agassiz Fuertes* (New York: Oxford University Press, 1956), pp. 307–308.

3. Letter to LAF from Elliott Coues, 21 November 1896; OL/CU.

4. From a handwritten autobiographical manuscript; OL/CU, (later published in *Amateur Sportsman*, September 1910).

5. *Ibid.*

6. *Ibid.*

7. Letter to Wilfred H. Osgood from LAF, 18 March 1918; OL/CU.

8. Letter to Witmer Stone from LAF, 22 November 1909; ANSP.

9. Letter to Bruce Horsfall from LAF, 9 March 1918; OL/CU.

10. Letter to Francis H. Herrick from LAF. 7 February 1916; OL/CU.

11. Letter to George Miksch Sutton from LAF, 15 February 1915; OL/CU.

12. Mary Fuertes Boynton, *Louis Agassiz Fuertes*, p. 5.

13. Quoted by Frank M. Chapman in "In Memoriam: Louis Agassiz Fuertes, 1874–1927," *The Auk*, January 1928, p. 3.

14. *Ibid.*, p. 4.

15. *Ibid.*, p. 6.

16. Two months after Fuertes' death, a memorial service was held in Willard Straight Hall at Cornell University. When asked to cite a precedent for such an event, Cornell president Livingston Farrand responded by saying, "There is no precedent for Fuertes." For this and other references to Fuertes' unique qualities, see Mary Fuertes Boynton, *Louis Agassiz Fuertes*, pp. 39, 307.

17. Letter to Mrs. E. A. Fuertes from Elliott Coues, 29 March 1897; OL/CU.

18. Letter to LAF from Abbott Thayer, 15 December 1896; OL/CU.

19. Letter to LAF from Abbott Thayer, 24 March 1897; OL/CU.

20. Letter to LAF from Abbott Thayer, 9 May 1897; OL//CU.

21. *Ibid.*

22. Letter to Mrs. Abbott Thayer from LAF, 3 March 1917; OL/CU.

23. Letter to LAF from Abbott Thayer, 11 May 1897; OL/CU.

24. Letter to John Paul Young from LAF, 11 December 1897; OL/CU.

25. Letter to Frank M. Chapman from LAF, 7 January 1911; OL/CU.

26. Letter to D. C. Davis, Director of the Field Museum, from LAF, 23 April 1926; FMNH.

27. Newspaper fragment, Fuertes Collection, OL/CU.

28. Letter to Mr. and Mrs. E. A. Fuertes from LAF, June 1899; OL/CU.

29. Letter to Mr. and Mrs. E. A. Fuertes from LAF, May 1899; OL/CU.

30. Letter to Mr. and Mrs. E. A. Fuertes from LAF, 31 May 1899; OL/CU.

31. Alton A. Lindsey, "The Harriman Alaska Expedition of 1899," *BioScience* 28, no. 6 (June, 1978): 384.

32. Vernon Bailey, "Recollections of Louis Agassiz Fuertes," original manuscript, OL/CU; quoted in Mary F. Boynton, *Louis Agassiz Fuertes*, p. 64.

33. Letter to Mrs. E. A. Fuertes from LAF, 29 May 1901; OL/CU.

34. Letter to the Abbott Thayer family from LAF, 1 September 1905; OL/CU.

35. Letter to George Miksch Sutton from LAF, 30 March 1915; OL/CU.

36. Letter to George Miksch Sutton from LAF, 15 February 1915; OL/CU.

37. Roger Tory Peterson, "Bird Painting in America," *Audubon Magazne*, May/June 1942, p. 169.

38. Letter to LAF from Frank M. Chapman 27 February 1901; OL/CU.

39. Letter to Gilbert Grosvenor from LAF, 24 June 1918; OL/CU.

40. Letter to Mary Fuertes Boynton from Allan Brooks, 28 February 1942; OL/CU.

41. Letter to Allan Brooks from LAF, 30 October 1921; OL/CU.

42. Letter to Gilbert Grosvenor from LAF, 3 January 1924; OL/CU.

43. Letter to LAF from H. S. Morgan, Forbes Lithograph Manufacturing Co., 29 December 1923; OL/CU.

44. Frank M. Chapman, remarks made at Fuertes Memorial Service, Cornell University 30 October 1927; quoted in Mary Fuertes Boynton, *Louis Agassiz Fuertes*, pp. 307–308.

PART II

1. The earliest comparison between the two artists was made by Elliott Coues in a book review of Florence A. Merriam's *A-Birding on a Bronco* (1896), which was published in *New York Nation*, 12 November 1896. A more comprehensive discussion may be found in Frank M. Chapman's "Fuertes and Audubon: A Comparison of the Work and Personalities of Two of the World's Greatest Bird Artists," *Natural History*, March 1937.

2. From a handwritten autobiographical manuscript; OL/CU (later published in *Amateur Sportsman*, September 1910).

3. Letter to Keith Shaw Williams from LAF, 26 May 1921; OL/CU.

4. Letter to LAF from Elliott Coues, 12 June 1895; quoted in Frank M. Chapman, "In Memoriam: Louis Agassiz Fuertes, 1874–1927," p. 8.

5. Letter to LAF from Elliott Coues, 14 November 1895; OL/CU.

6. Elliott Coues, book review, *New York Nation,* 12 November 1896.

7. Letter to LAF from Elliott Coues, 14 September 1896, OL/CU.

8. Letter to LAF from Elliott Coues, 21 November 1896, quoted by Frank M. Chapman in "In Memoriam: Louis Agassiz Fuertes, 1874–1927," p. 11.

9. Letter to LAF from Elliott Coues, 6 February 1897, quoted by Frank M. Chapman, *ibid,* p. 12.

10. Letter to LAF from Elliott Coues, quoted in Mary Fuertes Boynton, *Louis Agassiz Fuertes,* p. 12.

11. Letter to LAF from Elliott Coues, 22 July 1897; OL/CU.

12. LAF autobiographical manuscript, *op. cit.*

13. Letter to LAF from Abbott Thayer. 9, May 1897; OL/CU.

14. This description comes from Louis Fuertes' sister Kippy, who also spent time with the Thayers. For a more complete description, see Mary Fuertes Boynton, *Louis Agassiz Fuertes,* p. 27.

15. Letter to Mary Fuertes Boynton from Gladys Thayer Reasoner, 10 November 1941; OL/CU.

16. Letter to George Miksch Sutton from LAF, 30 March 1915; OL/CU.

17. Letter to Keith Shaw Williams from LAF, 4 December 1922; OL/CU.

18. Letter to George Miksch Sutton from LAF, 30 March 1915; OL/CU.

19. Letter to John Paul Young from LAF, 11 December 1897; OL/CU.

20. Letter to LAF from Abbott Thayer, 3 May 1898; OL/CU.

21. *Ibid.*

22. Frank M. Chapman, "A Great Portrait Painter of Birds," *American Museum Journal,* 15, no. 5 (May 1915): 221.

23. Frank M. Chapman, "In Memoriam: Louis Agassiz Fuertes, 1874–1927," p. 23.

24. Wilfred Hudson Osgood, "Louis Agassiz Fuertes," *Science* 66 18 November 1927): 6.

25. Letter to LAF from Abbott Thayer, 21 November 1898; OL/CU.

26. Letter to LAF from Abbott Thayer, n.d., Fall 1898; OL/CU.

27. Letter to LAF from Elliott Coues, 31 January 1899; OL/CU.

28. Letter to LAF from Elliott Coues, 16 May 1899; OL/CU.

29. Letter to LAF from Frank M. Chapman, 8 September 1902; AMNH.

30. Letter to Mrs. E. A. Fuertes from LAF, 18 April 1901; OL/CU.

31. Letter to Fuertes family from LAF, 29 April 1901; OL/CU.

32. Letter to Fuertes family from LAF, 23 May 1901; OL/CU.

33. *Ibid.*

34. Letter to Fuertes family from LAF, 29 April 1901; OL/CU.

35. Letter to LAF from Abbott Thayer, 9 May 1897; OL/CU.

36. Letter to LAF from Caspar Whitney, 27 March 1901; OL/CU.

37. Letter to Joseph Grinnell from LAF, 7 July 1918; OL/CU.

38. Letter to Keith Shaw Williams from LAF, n.d., 1921 or 1922; OL/CU.

39. Letter to Frank M. Chapman from LAF, 21 June 1918; OL/CU.

40. Letter to LAF from Gilbert Grosvenor, 31 August 1918; OL/CU.

41. Letter to Gilbert Grosvenor from LAF, 2 September 1918; OL/CU.

42. Letter to Frank M. Chapman from LAF, 18 September 1918; OL/CU.

43. Letter to A. K. Fisher from LAF, 19 August 1915; OL/CU.

44. Letter to A. K. Fisher from LAF, 10 August 1915; OL/CU.

45. Letter to Frank D. Blair from LAF, 31 January 1926; OL/CU.

46. Letter to Frank M. Chapman from LAF, 29 December 1911; OL/CU.

47. Letter to Allan Brooks from LAF, September 1921; OL/CU.

48. Letter to LAF from Frank M. Chapman, 17 December 1912; private collection.

49. Letter to Witmer Stone from LAF, December 1912; private collection.

50. Letter to LAF from Witmer Stone, 21 December 1912; private collection.

51. Letter to LAF from Witmer Stone, 21 November 1914; private collection.

52. Letter to Gilbert Grosvenor from LAF, 8 April 1918; OL/CU.

53. Although Fuertes only made one original clay sculpture, he had the piece cast in multiple pairs to be used as bookends. A pair were exhibited in the Pennsylvania Academy of the Fine Arts' 120th Annual Exhibition in 1925.

54. Letter to Wilfred H. Osgood from LAF, 17 April 1926; OL/CU.

55. Letter to T. Gilbert Pearson from LAF, 5 October 1921; OL/CU.

56. Arthur Augustus Allen, "The Passing of a Great Teacher: Louis Agassiz Fuertes," *Bird-Lore* 29 (September 1927).

57. Letter to Wilfred H. Osgood from LAF, 15 November 1923; OL/CU.

58. Letter to Stanley Field from LAF, 29 August 1926; FMNH.

59. Letter to Madge Fuertes from LAF, 12 November 1926: OL/CU.

60. Letter to George Miksch Sutton from LAF, 26 June 1927; OL/CU.

61. Mary Fuertes Boynton, *Louis Agassiz Fuertes,* p. 306.

62. Letter to Conrad Roland from LAF, 15 September 1925; OL/CU.

63. Letter to Abbott Thayer from LAF, April 1916; OL/CU.

64. *Ibid.*

65. Letter to the author from Terrance Shortt, 7 December 1981.

66. Letter to George Miksch Sutton from LAF, 21 January 1916; OL/CU.

67. George Miksch Sutton, *To a Young Bird Artist: Letters from Louis Agassiz Fuertes to George Miksch Sutton.* (Norman: University of Oklahoma Press, 1979), p. 83.

68. Roger Tory Peterson, Introduction, *Louis Agassiz Fuertes and the Singular Beauty of Birds* (New York: Harper & Row, 1971).

69. Letter to Mary Fuertes Boynton from George Miksch Sutton, 3 November 1949; OL/CU.

PART III

1. Letter to Frank M. Chapman from LAF, n.d., 1911; OL/CU.

2. LAF autobiographical manuscript, OL/CU; later published in *Amateur Sportsman,* September 1910.

3. *Ibid.*

4. John Burroughs, "Narrative of the Expedition," *Alaska: The Harriman Alaska Expedition Report* (New York: Doubleday, Page, 1901), pp. 17–18.

5. Letter to Fuertes' family from LAF, 1 June 1899; OL/CU.

6. Letter to Fuertes' family from LAF, June 1899; OL/CU.

7. *Ibid.*

8. Letter to Fuertes' family from LAF, 1, June 1899; OL/CU.

9. Letter to Fuertes' family from LAF, June 1899 (letter no. 4); OL/CU.

10. John Burroughs, "Narrative of the Expedition," p. 40.

11. Letter to Fuertes' family from LAF, 10 June 1899; OL/CU.

12. Letter to Mrs. John Muir from John Muir, 14 June 1899, published in William Frederic Bade, *The Life and Letters of John Muir* (Boston: Houghton Mifflin, 1924), p. 325.

13. Letter to Fuertes' family from LAF, 10 July 1899; OL/CU.

14. Letter to Fuertes' family from LAF, 18 July 1899; OL/CU.

15. *Ibid.*

16. Letter to Fuertes' family from LAF, 31 July 1899; OL/CU.

17. John Burroughs, "Narrative of the Expedition," p. 118.

18. Letter to Mary and Cornelia Harriman, Elizabeth Averell, and Dorothea Draper from John Muir, published in William Frederic Bade, *The Life and Letters of John Muir,* pp. 329–330.

19. Letter to Fuertes' family from LAF, 31 July 1899; OL/CU.

20. Letter to A. K. Fisher from LAF, 1 Janurary 1900; OL/CU.

21. Letter to Fuertes' family from LAF, 13 April 1901; OL/CU.

22. *Ibid.*

23. Letter to Mrs. E. A. Fuertes from LAF, 18 April 1901; OL/CU.

24. *Ibid.*

25. Letter to Mrs. E. A. Fuertes from LAF, 20 April 1901; OL/CU.

26. *Ibid.*

27. *Ibid.*

28. Letter to Fuertes' family from LAF, 29 April 1901; OL/CU.

29. Letter to Mr. and Mrs. E. A. Fuertes from LAF, 8 May 1901; OL/CU.

30. Letter to Mr. and Mrs. E. A. Fuertes from LAF, 16 May 1901; OL/CU.

31. Letter to Fuertes' family from LAF, 9 June 1901; OL/CU.

32. *Ibid.*

33. Letter to Fuertes' family from LAF, 15 June 1901; OL/CU.

34. Letter to Fuertes' family from LAF, n.d., May or June 1901; OL/CU.

35. Letter to Fuertes' family from LAF, 24 July 1901; OL/CU.

36. *Ibid.*

37. Frank M. Chapman, *Camps and Cruises of an Ornithologist* (New York: Appleton, 1908), p. 155.

38. *Ibid.*

39. Letter to Abbott Thayer from LAF, 3 June 1902; OL/CU.

40. Letter to LAF from William Hornaday, 13 May 1921; OL/CU.

41. Letter to Madge Fuertes from LAF, 17 August 1909; OL/CU.

42. Letter to Madge Fuertes from LAF, 21 March 1910; OL/CU.

43. Letter to Madge Fuertes from LAF, 28 March 1910; OL/CU.

44. *Ibid.*

45. *Ibid.*

46. Postcard to Madge Fuertes from LAF, n.d., between 28 March and 9 April 1910; OL/CU.

47. Letter to Madge Fuertes from LAF, 9 April 1910.

48. The new discovery was reported in *The Auk,* January 1911.

49. Frank M. Chapman, *My Tropical Air Castle* (New York: Appleton, 1929).

50. Letter to Wilfred H. Osgood from LAF, 12 September 1923; OL/CU.

51. Letter to Madge Fuertes from LAF, 28 March 1911; OL/CU.

52. Letter to Madge Fuertes from LAF, 31 March 1911; OL/CU.

53. Letter to Madge Fuertes from LAF, 5 April 1911; OL/CU.

54. Letter to Madge Fuertes from LAF, April 1911; OL/CU.

55. Letter to Madge Fuertes from LAF, 26 April 1911; OL/CU.

56. Letter to Madge Fuertes from LAF, 24 April 1911; OL/CU.

57. Letter to Madge Fuertes from LAF, 26 January 1913; OL/CU.

58. *Ibid.*

59. Letter to Madge Fuertes from LAF, 9 February 1913; OL/CU.

60. Letter to Madge Fuertes from LAF, 16 February 1913; OL/CU.

61. Letter to Madge Fuertes from LAF, 28 February 1913; OL/CU.

62. *Ibid.*

63. Wilfred Hudson Osgood, "Louis Agassiz Fuertes," p. 472.

64. Letter to Frank M. Chapman, 18 September 1918; OL/CU.

65. Letter to LAF from James E. Baum, 17 March 1926; OL/CU.

66. Letter to LAF from Wilfred H. Osgood, 15 April 1926; OL/CU.

67. Telegram to LAF from James E. Baum, 16 April 1926; OL/CU.

68. Letter to Wilfred H. Osgood from LAF, 17 April 1926; OL/CU.

69. Letter to Madge Fuertes from LAF, 8 October 1926; OL/CU.

70. James E. Baum, *Savage Abyssinia* (New York: J. H. Sears, 1927), pp. 18–19.

71. Alfred M. Bailey, "With Louis Fuertes in Abyssinia," *The Living Bird, (Sixteenth Annual) 1977* (Ithaca, N.Y.: Cornell University, Laboratory of Ornithology, 1977), p. 106.

72. Letter to Madge Fuertes from LAF, 11 October 1926; OL/CU.

73. James E. Baum, *Savage Abyssinia,* p. 46.

74. Alfred M. Bailey, "With Louis Fuertes in Abyssinia," p. 107.

75. Letter to Madge Fuertes from LAF, 11 October 1926; OL/CU.

76. Alfred M. Bailey, "With Louis Fuertes in Abyssinia," p. 106.

77. Letter to Madge Fuertes from LAF, 21 October 1926; OL/CU.

78. James E. Baum, original typescript, 30 October 1926; FMNH.

79. Letter to Madge and Mary Fuertes from LAF, 20 January 1927; OL/CU.

80. Letter to Frank M. Chapman from LAF, 23 January 1927; OL/CU

81. James E. Baum, *Savage Abyssinia,* p. 44.

82. Alfred M. Bailey, "With Louis Fuertes in Abyssinia," p. 116.

83. *Ibid.,* p. 118.

84. *Ibid.,* p. 121.

85. Letter to LAF from Wilfred H. Osgood, 20 July 1927, OL/CU.

86. Alfred M. Bailey, manuscript field journal, 1 May 1927, p. 115; FMNH.

87. Letter to Sumner Fuertes from LAF, 7 May 1927; OL/CU.

88. Alfred M. Bailey, manuscript field journal, May 1927; FMNH.

89. Frank M. Chapman, "Louis Agassiz Fuertes," *Bird-Lore,* September 1927.

Selected Bibliography

Album of Abyssinian Birds and Mammals from Paintings by Louis Agassiz Fuertes. Introduction by Wilfred Hudson Osgood. Chicago: Field Museum of Natural History, 1930.

ALLEN, ARTHUR AUGUSTUS. "The Passing of a Great Teacher: Louis Agassiz Fuertes." *Bird-Lore* 29 (September 1927): 372–376.

BADE, WILLIAM FREDERIC. *The Life and Letters of John Muir,* 2 vols. Boston: Houghton Mifflin, 1924.

BAILEY, ALFRED M. "With Louis Fuertes in Abyssinia." *The Living Bird (Sixteenth Annual),* 1977. Ithaca, N.Y.: Cornell University, Laboratory of Ornithology, 1977, pp. 103–122.

BARRUS, CLARA. *The Life and Letters of John Burroughs.* Boston: Houghton Mifflin 1925.

BAUM, JAMES. *Savage Abyssinia.* New York: J. H. Sears, 1927.

———. *Unknown Ethiopia.* New York: Grosset & Dunlap, 1935.

BOYNTON, MARY FUERTES. "Fuertes Remembered." *Frontiers Annual.* Philadelphia: The Academy of Natural Sciences of Philadelphia, 1979, pp. 59–64.

———. *Louis Agassiz Fuertes.* New York: Oxford University Press, 1956.

———. "Louis Agassiz Fuertes." *New York State Conservationist* 7, no. 4 (1954): 10–12.

BROOKS, PAUL. *Speaking for Nature.* Boston: Houghton Mifflin, 1980.

BURROUGHS, JOHN; MUIR, JOHN; GRINNELL, GEORGE BIRD ET AL. *Alaska: The Harriman Alaska Expedition Report.* New York: Doubleday, Page, 1901.

CHAPMAN, FRANK M. *Autobiography of a Bird Lover.* New York: Appleton, 1933.

———. *Camps and Cruises of an Ornithologist.* New York: Appleton, 1908.

———. "Fuertes and Audubon: A Comparison of the Work and Personalities of Two of the World's Greatest Bird Artists." *Natural History* 42 (1937): 205–213.

———. "A Great Portrait Painter of Birds." *Bird-Lore* 17 (1915): 277–284.

———. "In Memoriam: Louis Agassiz Fuertes, 1874–1927," *The Auk* 45 (1928): 1–26.

———. "Louis Agassiz Fuertes, 1874–1927." *Bird-Lore* 29 (1927): 359–368.

———. "Memories of Louis Fuertes." *Bird-Lore* 41 (1939): 3–10.

———. *My Tropical Air Castle.* New York: Appleton, 1929.

CLARKE, JAMES MITCHELL. *The Life and Adventures of John Muir.* San Francisco: Sierra Club Books, 1980.

CUTRIGHT, PAUL RUSSELL, AND BRODHEAD, MICHAEL J. *Elliott Coues, Naturalist and Frontier Historian.* Urbana: University of Illinois Press, 1981.

DRAHOS, NICK. "Early Fuertes Paintings Come Home." *Conservationist* 22 (1968): 26–27.

ECKELBERRY, DON RICHARD. "Birds in Art and Illustration." *The Living Bird (Second Annual),* 1963. Ithaca, N.Y.: Cornell University, Laboratory of Ornithology, 1963, pp. 69–82.

FUERTES, LOUIS AGASSIZ. "Impressions of the Voices of Tropical Birds." *Bird-Lore* (1913): 341–344; 16 (1914): 1–4, 96–101, 161–169, 342–349, 421–428.

FUERTES, LOUIS AGASSIZ, AND OSGOOD, WILFRED HUDSON. *Artist and Naturalist in Ethiopia.* Garden City, N.Y.: Doubleday, Doran, 1936.

HADLEY, ALDEN H. "With Fuertes in Florida." *American Forests* 37 (1931): 71–73, 128.

HANLEY, WAYNE. *Natural History in America.* New York: Quadrangle/New York Times, 1977.

HARRIMAN, E. ROLAND. *I Reminisce.* Garden City, N.Y.: Doubleday, 1975.

HOWES, PAUL GRISWOLD. *Photographer in the Rain-Forests.* Chicago: Paul G. Howes and Associates, Adams Press, 1969.

KENNAN, GEORGE. *E. H. Harriman, A Biography,* 2 vols. Boston: Houghton Mifflin, 1922.

LAING, HAMILTON M. *Allan Brooks: Artist Naturalist.* Vancouver: British Columbia Provincial Museum Special Publication No. 3, 1979.

LINDSEY, ALTON A. "The Harriman Alaska Expedition of 1899." *BioScience* 28, no. 6 (June 1978): 383–386.

MARCHAM, FREDERICK GEORGE. *Louis Agassiz Fuertes and the Singular Beauty of Birds.* New York: Harper & Row, 1971.

———. "Louis Fuertes Revisited." *The Living Bird (Second Annual), 1963.* Ithaca, N.Y.: Cornell University, Laboratory of Ornithology, 1963, pp. 83–92.

MENGEL, ROBERT M. "Beauty and the Beast: Natural History and Art." *The Living Bird (Eighteenth Annual) 1979–80.* Ithaca, N.Y.: Cornell University Laboratory of Ornithology, 1979–1980, pp. 27–70.

MUIR, JOHN. *Edward Henry Harriman.* Garden City, N.Y.: Doubleday, Page, 1916.

NORELLI, MARTINA R. *American Wildlife Painting.* New York: Watson-Guptill Publications, 1975.

OSGOOD, WILFRED HUDSON. "Louis Agassiz Fuertes." *Science* 66 (1927): 469–472.

PALMER, EPHRAIM LAWRENCE. "Louis Agassiz Fuertes." *Nature Magazine* 12 (1928): 177–179.

SAMSON, JOHN G., ed. *The Worlds of Ernest Thompson Seton.* New York: Knopf, 1976.

SETON, ERNEST THOMPSON. *Trail of an Artist-Naturalist.* New York: Charles Scribner's Sons, 1940.

SHERWOOD, MORGAN B. *Exploration of Alaska 1865-1900.* New Haven: Yale University Press, 1965.

STERLING, KEIR B. *Last of the Naturalists: The Career of C. Hart Merriam.* New York: Arno Press, 1977.

———. *Selected Works of Clinton Hart Merriam.* New York: Arno Press, 1974.

SUTTON, GEORGE MIKSCH. *Bird Student: An Autobiography.* Austin: University of Texas Press, 1980.

———. "Fuertes and the Young Bird Artist." *Audubon Magazine* 44 (1942): 37–40.

———. "Fuertes Remembered." *Audubon Magazine* 76, no. 6 (November 1974): 58–67.

———. "Louis Fuertes at Work." *Audubon Magazine* 44 (1942): 37–40.

———. "Louis Fuertes, Teacher." *Audubon Magazine* 42 (1941): 521–524.

———. *To a Young Bird Artist: Letters from Louis Agassiz Fuertes to George Miksch Sutton.* Norman: University of Oklahoma Press, 1979.

WELLS, DAVID I. "Drawing Wild Birds in Their Native Haunts; A Sketch of the Personality and Methods of Louis Agassiz Fuertes, the Bird Artist," *Outing Magazine* 54 (1909): 565–573.

Red-breasted Merganser
Mergus serrator
Ink wash
9½" × 11½"

Index

A-Birding on a Bronco (Merriam), 8, 12,
Abyssinian expedition, 92–93, 139–58, 167
Academy of Natural Sciences of
   Philadelphia, The, ix, xii, xiii, 4, 67, 80,
   165, 168
African Birds of Prey (Brown), 167
Agassiz, Louis, 2
Alaska expedition, 12–14, 16, 52, 59, 61,
   99–108
Albasso, Mt., 92
Alberta, 120
*Album of Abyssinian Birds and Mammals from
   Paintings by Louis Agassiz Fuertes,* 167
Allen, Arthur, 90
Amateur Sportsman magazine, 3
American Birds, 168
"American Birds of Prey—A Review of
   Their Value," 77
"American Game Birds," 168
American Museum of Natural History, x,
   1, 24, 80, 85, 90, 117, 118–19, 120, 128,
   129, 135, 165–66
American Ornithologists' Union (AOU),
   xi, 1, 8–10, 12, 14, 24, 28, 30, 32, 36, 39,
   41, 55, 61, 80–82, 84, 95, 101, 120
American Ornithology (Wilson), 4
Arm and Hammer Baking Soda, 22, 46,
   89, 167
Artist and Naturalist in Ethiopia (Osgood),
   167
Audubon, John James, ix, xii, xiii, 1, 4, 5,
   7, 27, 28, 32, 45, 52, 59
"Audubon Art Tours," 168
Audubon groups, 90
Auk, The, 9, 81, 82, 84–85

Bahamas, 107, 116–18
Bailey, Alfred M., 145, 146, 148–49, 153,
   155, 156, 158
Bailey, Florence Merriam, 8, 12, 30, 31,
   53, 70, 116
Bailey, Liberty Hyde, 6–7
Bailey, Vernon, 14, 15, 63–64, 70, 108,
   111, 113, 114, 116

Baum, James E. (Jack), 139, 141–42, 145,
   149, 153, 154, 156
Beebe, William, 22, 89, 119
Bent, Arthur Cleveland, 120
Birdcraft (Wright), 53
Bird Life of Texas, The (Oberholser), 165
Bird-Lore, 1, 24, 30, 56, 90, 138, 158, 161,
   166, 167
Birds of America, The (Audubon), 4
Birds of America (Pearson, ed.), 168
Birds of Eastern North America (Chapman),
   24
*Birds of Massachusetts and Other New
   England States* (Forbush), xii, 24, 25, 89,
   92, 167
Birds of New York, The (Eaton), xi, xii, 55,
   167, 168
Birds of the Rockies (Keyser), 53
"Birds of Town and Country," 168
Bishop, Richard E., 166
Black Phoebe, 16
Bonhote: J. Lewis, 117–18; Mrs. J. Lewis,
   117
Boston Museum of Science, 167
Boston Society of Natural History, 167
Boynton, Mary Fuertes, x, 19, 93, 158,
   166
Boy Scouts of America, 22, 23–24, 139
Brandreth, Courtenay, xi, 95, 166
Brasher, 24
Brett, Mr., 35
Brewer's blackbird, 49
Brooks, Allan, 24, 25, 78
Brown, Leslie, 167
Bull, Charles Livingston, xi, 67, 70
Burgess, Thornton, 22, 89
Burgess Animal Book for Children, The, 89
Burgess Bird Book for Children, The, 89
Burroughs, John, 12–14, 22, 100, 104, 107

California, University of; Museum of
   Vertebrate Zoology, 70, 72
Camps and Cruises of an Ornithologist
   (Chapman), 116–17

Cayuga, Lake, 21, 96
Chapman: Frank, 1, 12, 22–25, 30–31, 53,
   56, 74, 77–78, 81, 92, 116–17, 119–20,
   123–24, 126, 128–29, 131, 135–36,
   138–39, 161, 165–67; Mrs. Frank, 25,
   117
Charles Scribner's Sons, 166
Cherrie, George K., 136
Chicago Daily News, 24, 142, 167
Chisos Mountains, 113–14
Church, Charles T., 22
Church and Dwight Company, 22, 46, 89,
   167
Citizen Bird (Coues and Wright), 9, 33, 36,
   42, 52
Clark, James Lippit, 85
Cole, 103
Colombia, 128–38, 161
Coloration, concealing, 10–11, 38, 41–42,
   44, 74, 166, 167
"Coloration of Animals: The Basis for the
   Science of Camouflage," 90
Comstock, Anna, 6, 22
Cornell University, ix, 2, 6–8, 11–12,
   18–19, 27–28, 30–31, 67, 90, 165–67
Coues, Elliott, ix, 1–2, 8–10, 20, 27–30,
   32–36, 42, 50, 52, 53, 56
Country Gentleman, 22
Curtis, Edward S., 12, 103
Cuthbert Rookery, 120
Cutting, C. Suydam, 92, 145, 153, 156, 167

Dall, William H., 12
"Dash of environment" formula, 56
Davies, David Charles, 142
Davis Mountains, 114
Dioramas, 118–19, 128
Dublin, New Hampshire, 11, 36–37, 39, 42

Eaglesmere, 16, 18
Eaton, Elon Howard, xii, 55, 168
Eckstorm, Fannie Hardy, 53
Economic Value of Birds to the State
   (Chapman), 53

El Paso, 114, 116
Estrella, 117

"Falconry, the Sport of Kings," 77, 168
Farrand, Livingston, 90
Field, Stanley, 92, 142
Field Guide to the Birds (Peterson), 95
Field Museum of Natural History, 25, 46, 89, 92–93, 138, 141–42, 145, 151, 154, 156, 167
"Fifty Common Birds of Farm and Orchard," 165, 168
Finch, Mr. and Mrs. Dudley, 18
Fisher, A. K., 101, 103, 104, 107
Flamingo Hotel, Miami, 118–19
Flamingos, 118–19
Forbes Lithograph Manufacturing Company, 25
Forbush, Edward Howe, xii, 22, 24, 25, 89, 166, 167
Forest and Stream, 12
Fossey, Dian, 89
Fuertes, Estevan Antonio (father), 2, 6, 7, 18, 27, 35
Fuertes, James (brother), 6, 8
Fuertes, Louis Agassiz: Abyssinian studies, 92–93, 139–58, 167; advertising projects, 22, 46; Alaska trip, 12–14, 16, 52, 59, 61, 99–108; artistic concerns, 44–45, 70; artistic credo, 94; artistic strengths, 45, 50, 52, 70; authority on bird behavior, 78; autobiography, 3; Bahamas, in, 107, 116–18; birds of prey, and, 46, 70, 77–78; birth, 2; bookplates, 67, 77; California, to, 120; Canada trips, 120, 123, 161; career choice, 20, 27; caricatures, 7; childhood, 2, 11; childrens' books, 89; collage/paintings, 166; Colombia trips, 128–38, 161; Colorado, in, 120; commissions, 21–22, 30, 33, 53, 55, 70, 74, 77, 80–81, 89; compositions, 16, 42, 44; death, 25, 92, 158; distributors of illustrations, 22; earliest paintings, 3–5; education, 7–9, 30–31, 34–35; family, 2, 27; field observations, 11–16, 24, 44, 52, 61–64, 67, 78, 92, 99–161, 166; Florida trips, 44–45, 120; geometric designs, 67; home, 18, 21; honeymoon, 18, 120; influence of, 94–96; insect-eating birds, depictions of, 46–49; lectures, 46, 90; letters, 19, 165–66; live specimens, use of, 45–46, 80; marriage, 18; mediums, 85; memorial service, 25; Mexico, in, 107, 123–28, 161; naturalist, as, 99–161; Nevada trip, 120; New Mexico visit, 114, 116, 120; 1920s, in, 89, 92; obituary, 161; Oriental-art influence, 67; photographs, use of, 80–81, 166; poem by, 82; private versus commissioned works, 90; quotations from, 3–4, 19–20, 24–25, 28, 41–42, 62, 64, 74, 77–78, 80, 82, 86, 90, 92, 94, 96, 99, 101–5, 107–8,
111, 113–14, 118, 120, 124–26, 129–32, 135–39, 145–46, 148–49, 153, 156; sculpture, 85–86, 89, 166, 169; signature, change in, 52–53; song mimicry skills, 90, 138; studios, 21, 96, 100; style, 4–5, 16, 25, 52–53, 56, 59, 67; subjects, 3, 7, 11, 15–16, 49, 63–64, 67, 70, 72, 74, 77, 90; summers, 11, 16, 21, 36, 38–39; techniques, 28, 166; teenage years, 3–6; Texas, travel in, 15–16, 23, 52, 59, 61–64, 67, 113, 165, 167; on vermin control, 78; violence, attitude toward depicting, 46; World War I, during, 138–39
Fuertes, Margaret (Madge; wife), 18–19, 25, 72, 92, 120, 125, 153, 158, 165
Fuertes, Mary Katherine (Kippy; sister), 2, 5, 18, 19
Fuertes, Sumner (son), 19, 156
Fuertes Collection, 19, 166
Fuertes Room, 166
"Fuertes School," 96

Gannett, Henry, 103
George W. Elder (ship), 13, 101, 103–5, 107
Glacier Bay, 102–3, 104
Gojam province (Abyssinia), 155
Goshawk, 167
Gould, John, 7
Great Curassow, 80
Grinnell, George Bird, 12
Grinnell, Joseph, 70
Grosvenor, Gilbert, 23, 24, 70, 74, 77, 86, 168

Haile Selassie, 92, 145–46, 154
Hall Island, 105
Ham and Eggs (H.A.E) Club, 107
Handbook of Birds of Eastern North America (Chapman), 116
Handbook of Birds of the Western United States (Bailey, Florence Merriam), 53, 70, 116
Harriman, Averell, 100
Harriman: Edward Henry, 12–13, 52, 99, 104, 107; Mrs. Edward Henry, 102. *See also* Alaska expedition
Henrotin, Charles, 27
Herons of the United States (Pearson), 89
Hittell, Charles, 128
Hornaday, William, 119
Horned Owl, 167
Horsfall, Bruce, 4, 24, 128
Houghton Mifflin, 70
Howe, R. Heber, Jr., 9
Howes, Paul, 136–37

Icterus fuertesi (oriole), 126
"Impressions of the Voices of Tropical Birds," 138
Indian culture, 64, 67
Institute for Museum Services, 165

Irniger (Swiss painter), 7
Ithaca, New York, 2, 4, 5, 7, 18, 21, 24, 45, 96

Jamaica, 18, 120
Jaques, Francis Lee, xi, xii
"Jizz," the, xiii
Johnson, Walter Adams, 30

Kearny, 103
Kennedy Galleries, 90
Key to North American Birds (Coues), 28, 50, 52
Keyser, Leander S., 53
Kincaid, Edgar B., Jr., 165
Knight, Charles, xi, 44, 45, 72, 74, 77, 85, 99
Kuser, John Dryden, 96

"Larger North American Mammals, The," 21, 70, 96, 168
Leigh Yawkey-Woodson Art Museum, xii
Liljefors, Bruno, 96
Lindbergh, Charles, 158
Lizards, 64
Louis Agassiz Fuertes (Boynton), 93
Louis Agassiz Fuertes and the Singular Beauty of Birds (Marcham), 93–94, 167

Macmillan Company, 33
Magdelan Islands, 120
Magdalena River, 135
Mammals, 63–64, 70, 72, 74
Marcham, Frederick George, 93, 167
Massachusetts, Commonwealth of, 167
Maxon, William, 18
Merriam, C. Hart, 12, 14, 59, 61
Merriam, Florence A. *See* Bailey, Florence Merriam
Mexico, 107, 123–28, 161
Miller, Leo, 129
Miller, Olive Thorne, 53
Monograph of the Pheasants (Beebe), 89
Mountain gorillas, 86, 89
Muir, John, 12, 103–4, 107
Muir Glacier, 102–3
My Tropical Air Castle (Chapman), 128

National Audubon Society, 12, 167–68
National Geographic, 21–23, 70, 74, 77, 96, 145, 165, 168
National Geographic Society, The, 168
National Museum, 12
Natural History of Ducks, A (Phillips), 25, 89
"Naturalist Among the Mayan Ruins of Yucatan, A," 90
New York Nation, 32
New York State Forest, Fish, and Game Commission, 53, 56
New York State Museum, Albany, 168
New York Zoological Society, 119

Nichols, Hobart, 128
North American Fauna, 61

Oberholser, Harry C., 14, 16, 62–63, 108, 111, 113, 165
O'Connell, Geoffrey, 136
On the Birds' Highway (Howe), 9
Orioles, 126, 132, 161
Orizaba, Mt. (Citlaltepetl), 123–25
Ornithological Biography (Audubon), xii
Osgood, Wilfred Hudson, 46, 89, 138, 141–42, 145–46, 149, 151, 153, 156, 167
Osprey, The, 8, 30
"Our Common Dogs," 70, 74, 168
Outing, 22, 24, 70

Palmer, T. S., 165
Parkhurst, H. E., 9, 166
Patterson (assistant), 124
Pearson, T. Gilbert, 24, 89, 168
Pennsylvania Academy of the Fine Arts, 86
Perry, Mary, 2, 6, 8, 9, 18
Peterson, Roger Tory, ix, xi–xiii, 22, 95, 96
Philippines, 107
Phillips, John C., 25, 89
Pigments, transient, of birds, 99
Popoff Islands, 105

Ras Hailu, 155–56
Ras Tafari. *See* Haile Selassie
"Results of a Biological Survey of the San Francisco Mountain Region and Desert of the Little Colorado in Arizona" (Merriam, C. Hart), 61
Richardson, William, 129
Ridgway, Robert, 12, 101, 103
Ring, Thomas, 136
Rio Grande, 107, 111
Roland, Conrad, 94, 95
Rungius, Carl, 72, 74, 128

Sacramento Mountains, 114, 116
Sage, Mrs. Russell, 168
St. Nicholas, 22, 24
Sandys, Edwyn, 53
Sanford, Colonel D. A., 146, 148, 155
Sanford, Dr. and Mrs. Leonard C., 120
Saskatchewan, 120
Scarborough, New York, 39, 42, 49
Second Book of Birds, The (Miller), 53
Seton, Ernest Thompson, 22–24, 31
Settings, role in painting, 42, 44, 56, 59, 74
Sheldrake Point, 21, 96
Shortt, Terrance, 95
Sierra Club, 12
Singer, Arthur, xii
"Smaller North American Mammals, The," 23, 70, 74, 168
Smithsonian Institution, 6, 18, 52, 101, 107, 138
Song Birds and Water Fowl (Parkhurst), 9, 166
"Songs and Calls of Familiar Birds," 90
Stone, Witmer, 4, 82, 84–85, 165, 166
Strong, Walter, 141
Sumner, Margaret. *See* Fuertes, Margaret
Sutton, George Miksch, xii, 20, 21, 41, 92, 95–96, 166

Tampico, 125–26
Tannersville, New York, 92
Texas, biological survey of, 15–16, 23, 52, 59, 61–64, 67, 113, 165, 167
Texas Roadrunner, 16
Thayer, Abbott, 9–11, 18–20, 36–39, 41–42, 44–45, 49–50, 56, 67, 74, 78, 94, 96, 99, 104, 118, 166
Thayer, Emma, 39
Thayer, Gerald (Gra), 39, 44, 45, 49, 74, 99
Thayer, Gladys (Galla), 39
Thayer, Mary (Je-je), 39
"Thayeryland," 37

Thompson, Ernest Seton. *See* Seton, Ernest Thompson
Thorburn, Archibald, xi, 25, 96
To a Young Bird Artist; Letters from Louis Agassiz Fuertes to George Miksch Sutton, 96

Unadilla, New York, 25
Unalaska, 104
United States Biological Survey, xi, 12, 14, 24, 63, 101, 107, 165
United States Department of Agriculture, ix, 14–15, 49, 165; Bureau of Biological Survey, 61; Division of Economic Ornithology and Mammalogy, 59, 61
United States Fish and Wildlife Service, ix, 14, 165
Upland Game Birds (Sandys and Van Dyke), 53

Van Dyke, T. S., 53
Vermilion Flycatcher, 16
Vinegarroons, 15, 64
Vineyard Ranch, 116

"Warblers of North America, The," 168
Washington Academy of Sciences, 52, 107
Way to Study Birds, The (Kuser), 96
Whitney, Caspar, 70
Wilder, Burt, 6
Williams, Keith Shaw, 95
Wilson, Alexander, 4, 7, 45
Wolf, Joseph, 7, 35
Woodpeckers, The (Eckstorm), 53
Wright, Mabel Osgood, 9, 33, 53

Yucatan. *See* Mexico

Zone-tailed hawk, 15